JUMBLE®
GALAXY

A Universe of Challenging Puzzles

Henri Arnold
and
Mike Argirion

TRIUMPH
B O O K S

Copyright © 2011 by Tribune Media Services, Inc.
All rights reserved.

This book is available in quantity at special discounts
for your group or organization.

For further information, contact:

Triumph Books
814 North Franklin Street
Chicago, Illinois 60610

Printed in U.S.A.

ISBN: 978-1-60078-583-2

Design by Sue Knopf

CONTENTS

CLASSIC PUZZLES

DAILY PUZZLES

CHALLENGER PUZZLES

ANSWERS

JUMBLE® GALAXY

Classic Puzzles

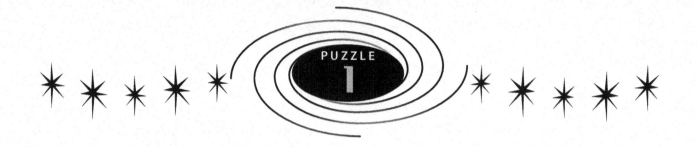
JUMBLE®

Unscramble these four Jumbles, one letter to each square, to form four ordinary words.

SONOW

DORIF

BOISHY

LABBUE

I'll be done in a minute

Take your time

WHAT THEY DID WHEN SHE PRESSED HIS SHIRT AND HE PRACTICED HIS SWING.

Now arrange the circled letters to form the surprise answer, as suggested by the above cartoon.

Answer here:

JUMBLE®

Unscramble these four Jumbles, one letter to each square, to form four ordinary words.

YAILG

CLUID

GATNIC

GUAJAR

It was love at first sight

He's old enough to be her father

THE ACCOUNTANT MARRIED HER RICH CLIENT BECAUSE SHE WAS----

Now arrange the circled letters to form the surprise answer, as suggested by the above cartoon.

Ans:

JUMBLE

Unscramble these four Jumbles, one letter to each square, to form four ordinary words.

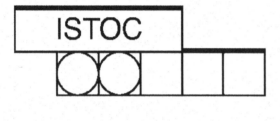

ISTOC

TINGY

THARGE

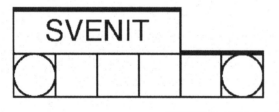

SVENIT

Where are my keys?

Don't move. I'll call a cab

WHAT THE BARTENDER TOLD THE TIPSY DRIVER TO DO.

Now arrange the circled letters to form the surprise answer, as suggested by the above cartoon.

Answer here:  "  "

JUMBLE®

Unscramble these four Jumbles, one letter to each square, to form four ordinary words.

OSOME

AFESH

FLYDON

GATHIL

Hey, you're leaving tracks. Get out!

WHAT SHE DID WHEN THE REPAIRMAN GOT DIRT ON HER CARPET.

Now arrange the circled letters to form the surprise answer, as suggested by the above cartoon.

Ans: ⬜⬜⬜⬜ ⬜⬜⬜ " ⬜⬜⬜ "

JUMBLE®

Unscramble these four Jumbles, one letter to each square, to form four ordinary words.

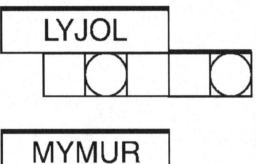

LYJOL

MYMUR

RUMMRU

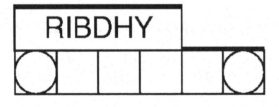

RIBDHY

Knock Knock

Who's there?

WHAT JUNIOR USED WHEN HE HELPED MOM WITH THE DISHES.

Now arrange the circled letters to form the surprise answer, as suggested by the above cartoon.

Answer here: " ◯◯◯ " ◯◯◯◯◯

JUMBLE®

Unscramble these four Jumbles, one letter to each square, to form four ordinary words.

COASH
⬜🔘🔘⬜🔘

STALN
🔘🔘⬜🔘🔘

CEPTID
⬜⬜🔘⬜🔘🔘

NURTUE
⬜⬜🔘🔘⬜🔘

I love
your outfit

WHAT SHE WORE TO
HER YOGA CLASS.

Now arrange the circled letters to form the surprise answer, as suggested by the above cartoon.

A: " 🔘🔘🔘🔘🔘🔘🔘 " 🔘🔘🔘🔘🔘

JUMBLE®

Unscramble these four Jumbles, one letter to each square, to form four ordinary words.

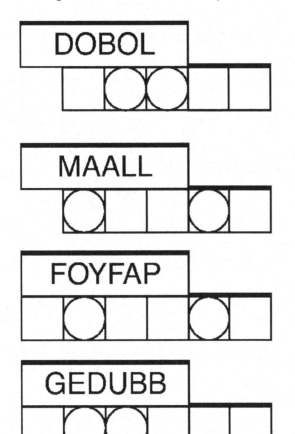

DOBOL

MAALL

FOYFAP

GEDUBB

It's been a long time since we met in Paris

WHAT IT CAN TAKE TO REKINDLE A ROMANCE.

Now arrange the circled letters to form the surprise answer, as suggested by the above cartoon.

Answer here: AN ⬡⬡⬡ ⬡⬡⬡⬡⬡

JUMBLE®

Unscramble these four Jumbles, one letter to each square, to form four ordinary words.

SYNIH

TRYAP

GINENE

LOUBES

Circumference, diameter, who cares?

FOR THE GEOMETRY CLASS, THE STUDY OF CIRCLES WAS——

Now arrange the circled letters to form the surprise answer, as suggested by the above cartoon.

Answer here: ◯◯◯◯◯◯◯◯◯

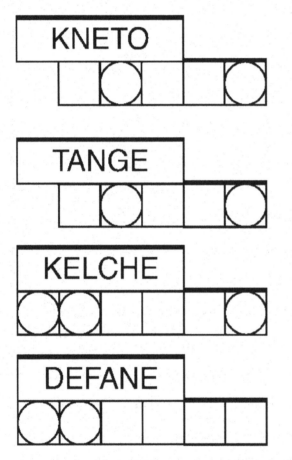

JUMBLE®

Unscramble these four Jumbles, one letter to each square, to form four ordinary words.

KNETO

TANGE

KELCHE

DEFANE

Whew, I'm a wreck

HEMMING DRESSES ALL DAY LEFT THE SEAMSTRESS----

Now arrange the circled letters to form the surprise answer, as suggested by the above cartoon.

Answer: ⬡⬡ ⬡⬡⬡ " ⬡⬡⬡⬡ "

JUMBLE®

Unscramble these four Jumbles, one letter to each square, to form four ordinary words.

OATAR

NEKIF

SAWURL

DOHOKE

Yeah, I'm glad to be back

He makes it sound routine

WHEN THE SPACE-CRAFT LANDED, THE ASTRONAUT WAS----

Now arrange the circled letters to form the surprise answer, as suggested by the above cartoon.

Ans: " ___ ___ ___ ___ " TO " ___ ___ ___ ___ ___ "

JUMBLE®

Unscramble these four Jumbles, one letter to each square, to form four ordinary words.

CRATT

HEMTY

ENZARB

ALESEW

You didn't hear it from me, but...

WHEN THE CLERK WHISPERED TO THE CUSTOMER OVER THE COUNTER, IT WAS---

Now arrange the circled letters to form the surprise answer, as suggested by the above cartoon.

Ans:

JUMBLE

Unscramble these four Jumbles, one letter to each square, to form four ordinary words.

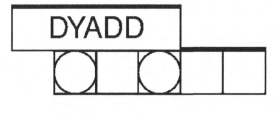

DYADD

WAKOE

GUTONE

CRADOC

This is an iron clad right of ownership

WHAT THE LAWYER DID FOR THE HOUSE BUYERS.

Now arrange the circled letters to form the surprise answer, as suggested by the above cartoon.

Answer: A ⬜⭕⭕⭕⭕ " ⭕⭕⭕⭕ "

JUMBLE®

Unscramble these four Jumbles, one letter to each square, to form four ordinary words.

MENOG

CHARN

BOUFLE

GLIMYR

You'll be the daughter

WHAT ROLE DID THE CHILD ACTRESS PLAY IN THE MOVIE?

Now arrange the circled letters to form the surprise answer, as suggested by the above cartoon.

Answer: A "⬡⬡⬡⬡⬡⬡" ⬡⬡⬡

JUMBLE®

Unscramble these four Jumbles, one letter to each square, to form four ordinary words.

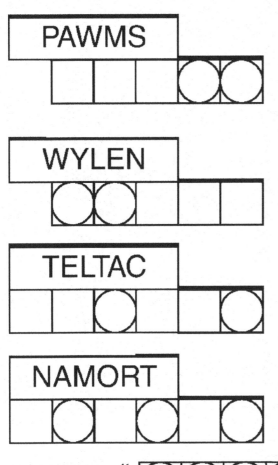

PAWMS

WYLEN

TELTAC

NAMORT

$200?

Those curls take a lot of time

WHEN THE HAIR-DRESSER RAISED HER FEE, IT WAS----

Now arrange the circled letters to form the surprise answer, as suggested by the above cartoon.

Answer: " ◯◯◯◯◯◯◯◯◯ "

JUMBLE®

Unscramble these four Jumbles, one letter to each square, to form four ordinary words.

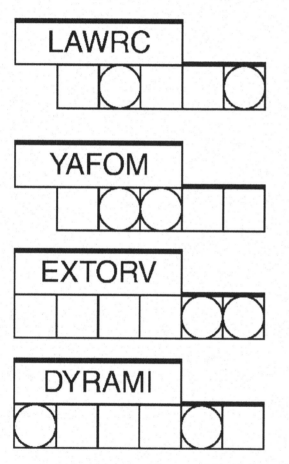

LAWRC

YAFOM

EXTORV

DYRAMI

You've got two cavities and...

WHAT THE COLLEGE STUDENT FACED WHEN HE WENT TO THE DENTIST.

Now arrange the circled letters to form the surprise answer, as suggested by the above cartoon.

Answer: AN "☐☐☐☐☐" ☐☐☐☐

JUMBLE

Unscramble these four Jumbles, one letter to
each square, to form four ordinary words.

NAGLD

RAMOJ

CAMBLE

WRALEY

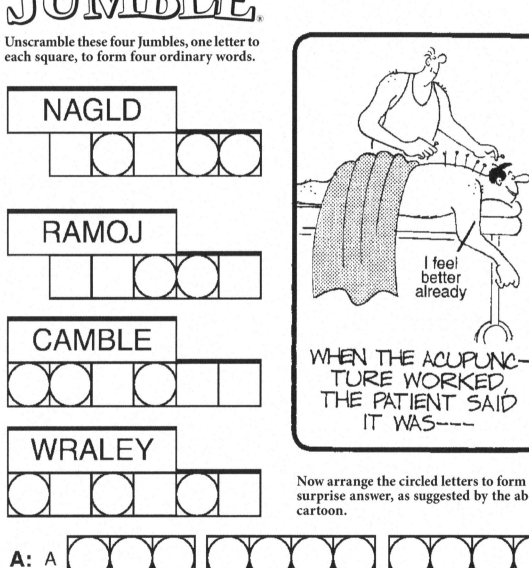

I feel
better
already

WHEN THE ACUPUNC-
TURE WORKED
THE PATIENT SAID
IT WAS----

Now arrange the circled letters to form the
surprise answer, as suggested by the above
cartoon.

A: A

JUMBLE®

Unscramble these four Jumbles, one letter to each square, to form four ordinary words.

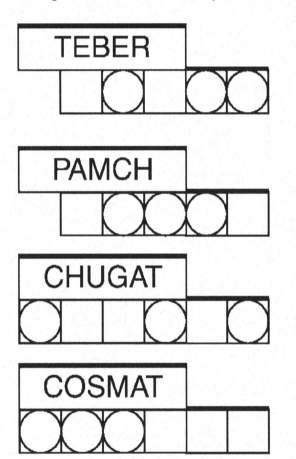

TEBER

PAMCH

CHUGAT

COSMAT

You played as good as you look

WHEN THE WINNING DOUBLES PARTNERS WORE THE SAME OUTFITS, IT WAS——

Now arrange the circled letters to form the surprise answer, as suggested by the above cartoon.

A: ☐☐☐☐☐ , ☐☐☐ , "☐☐☐☐☐"

JUMBLE®

Unscramble these four Jumbles, one letter to each square, to form four ordinary words.

RATIE

GHEED

YURSLE

CEDITE

Thanks for the lift

You shouldn't thumb a ride

WHAT THE GUIDANCE COUNSELOR DID WHEN HE PICKED UP THE HITCHHIKER.

Now arrange the circled letters to form the surprise answer, as suggested by the above cartoon.

A: " ⬡⬡⬡⬡⬡⬡⬡⬡ " HIM ⬡⬡⬡⬡⬡

JUMBLE®

Unscramble these four Jumbles, one letter to
each square, to form four ordinary words.

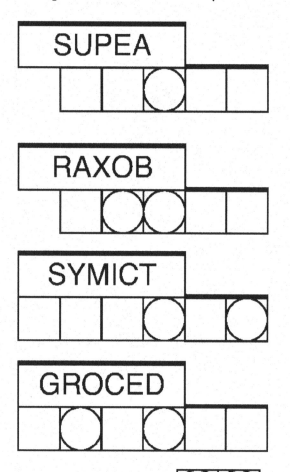

SUPEA

RAXOB

SYMICT

GROCED

Two-hour
recess

A JUDGE WILL DO
THIS WHEN HE HAS
A TENNIS MATCH.

Now arrange the circled letters to form the
surprise answer, as suggested by the above
cartoon.

Answer here: ⬡⬡ TO " ⬡⬡⬡⬡⬡ "

JUMBLE

Unscramble these four Jumbles, one letter to each square, to form four ordinary words.

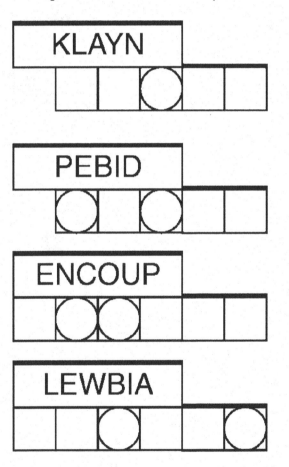

KLAYN

PEBID

ENCOUP

LEWBIA

WHAT THE SLEEP-
ING RECRUITS FELT
LIKE WHEN THEY
HEARD THE BUGLE.

Now arrange the circled letters to form the surprise answer, as suggested by the above cartoon.

Print answer here: ◯◯◯◯◯ " ◯◯ "

21

JUMBLE®

Unscramble these four Jumbles, one letter to each square, to form four ordinary words.

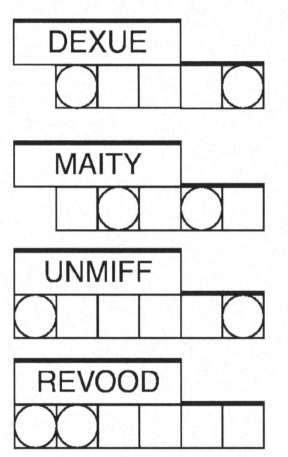

DEXUE

MAITY

UNMIFF

REVOOD

It sounds better over here

WHAT THE PIANO PLAYER WORKED ON.

Now arrange the circled letters to form the surprise answer, as suggested by the above cartoon.

Answer here: A " ⬡⬡⬡⬡⬡⬡⬡⬡ "

22

JUMBLE®

Unscramble these four Jumbles, one letter to each square, to form four ordinary words.

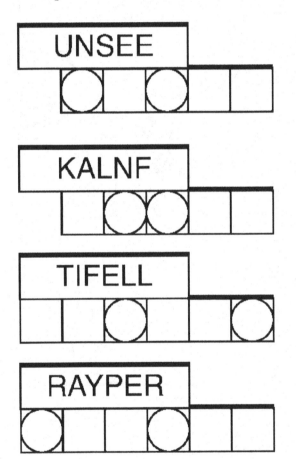

UNSEE

KALNF

TIFELL

RAYPER

WHAT HE SAW
WHEN HE VISITED
THE PRINT SHOP.

Now arrange the circled letters to form the surprise answer, as suggested by the above cartoon.

Answer here:  "  "

JUMBLE®

Unscramble these four Jumbles, one letter to each square, to form four ordinary words.

VANEH

UGOBS

FACEEF

GOFERR

He started it

No, he started it

WHAT THE BRAWLERS FACED WHEN THEY WERE ARRESTED FOR BATTERY.

Now arrange the circled letters to form the surprise answer, as suggested by the above cartoon.

Print answer here: "◯◯◯◯◯◯◯"

JUMBLE

Unscramble these four Jumbles, one letter to each square, to form four ordinary words.

PECOU

NEPOR

MEEDER

KATEIN

I'm bushed. Time to hit the sack

SO LONG, PAT

WHAT HE DID AFTER THE COMPANY FAREWELL PARTY.

Now arrange the circled letters to form the surprise answer, as suggested by the above cartoon.

Answer here: HE " ◯◯◯◯◯◯◯ "

JUMBLE®

Unscramble these four Jumbles, one letter to
each square, to form four ordinary words.

NIFET

NIMEC

BALMOG

NARXLY

My family will
be surprised

WHY MOM AGREED
TO APPEAR IN
THE MOVIE
CROWD SCENE.

Now arrange the circled letters to form the
surprise answer, as suggested by the above
cartoon.

A: FOR "〇〇〇〇〇" 〇〇〇〇〇

JUMBLE®

GALAXY

Daily Puzzles

JUMBLE®

Unscramble these four Jumbles, one letter to each square, to form four ordinary words.

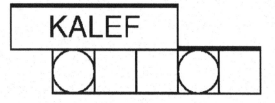

KALEF

KHECE

AJURAG

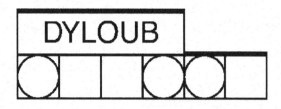

DYLOUB

It's missing something

Yeah, taste

THE CHEF'S NEW RECIPE FAILED BECAUSE IT WAS----

Now arrange the circled letters to form the surprise answer, as suggested by the above cartoon.

Answer here: ⬡⬡⬡⬡ - ⬡⬡⬡⬡⬡

28

JUMBLE®

Unscramble these four Jumbles, one letter to
each square, to form four ordinary words.

KORPE

HAFFC

SUTTRY

THORCC

You haven't missed
any meals, have
you, Angus

WHAT THE TAILOR
USED TO MEASURE
THE BAGPIPER
FOR HIS KILT.

Now arrange the circled letters to form the
surprise answer, as suggested by the above
cartoon.

Ans: " ⃝⃝⃝⃝⃝⃝⃝ " ⃝⃝⃝⃝⃝

JUMBLE®

Unscramble these four Jumbles, one letter to each square, to form four ordinary words.

KNACS

GAUVE

RYSLIG

PHARIS

BANK

We're short every month

WHAT HE USED ON A RAINY DAY.

Now arrange the circled letters to form the surprise answer, as suggested by the above cartoon.

Answer: ◯◯◯ ◯◯◯◯◯◯◯◯

30

JUMBLE®

Unscramble these four Jumbles, one letter to
each square, to form four ordinary words.

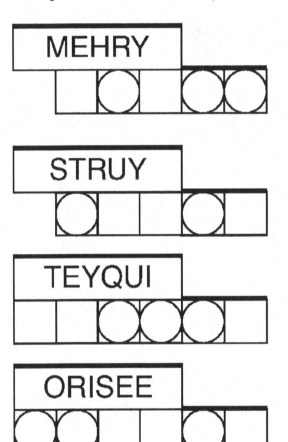

MEHRY

STRUY

TEYQUI

ORISEE

Who does he
think he is?

Wait'll he sees
his tip

WHAT AN "UPPITY"
WAITER IS BOUND
TO GET.

Now arrange the circled letters to form the
surprise answer, as suggested by the above
cartoon.

A: A " ◯◯◯◯◯ " ◯◯◯ OF ◯◯◯◯◯

JUMBLE®

Unscramble these four Jumbles, one letter to
each square, to form four ordinary words.

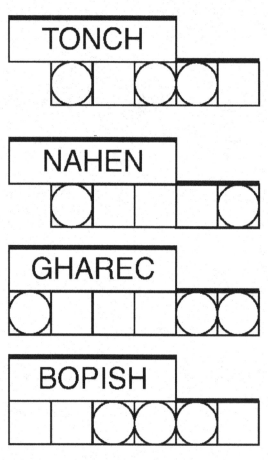

TONCH

NAHEN

GHAREC

BOPISH

How original. A
sheet with holes

WHEN HE ENTERED
THE COSTUME
CONTEST, HE
DIDN'T HAVE A----

Now arrange the circled letters to form the
surprise answer, as suggested by the above
cartoon.

A: " ☐☐☐☐☐☐ " OF A ☐☐☐☐☐☐☐

JUMBLE®

Unscramble these four Jumbles, one letter to each square, to form four ordinary words.

CDAYE

SYASA

DRAMOR

FLARTE

I need to refocus

How 'bout a beer and pizza

WHEN THE ASTRONOMY STU-DENTS FINISHED STUDYING, THEY WERE---

Now arrange the circled letters to form the surprise answer, as suggested by the above cartoon.

Ans: " ◯◯◯◯◯◯ " ◯◯◯◯

JUMBLE®

Unscramble these four Jumbles, one letter to
each square, to form four ordinary words.

KOHCE

KETOS

MISTUR

ERPICH

It's so expensive **OUCH!**

$200

WHAT SHE EXPERI-
ENCED WHEN SHE
SHOPPED FOR A
CACTUS PLANT.

Now arrange the circled letters to form the
surprise answer, as suggested by the above
cartoon.

A: " ⃝⃝⃝⃝⃝⃝⃝ " ⃝⃝⃝⃝⃝

JUMBLE

Unscramble these four Jumbles, one letter to each square, to form four ordinary words.

AGGUE

SABSY

NIPPOL

GAMIPE

WHY THE SENATOR DIDN'T SUBMIT HIS REPORT.

Now arrange the circled letters to form the surprise answer, as suggested by the above cartoon.

A: A " ◯◯◯◯ " WAS ◯◯◯◯◯◯◯

35

JUMBLE®

Unscramble these four Jumbles, one letter to each square, to form four ordinary words.

HYSYL

YANGO

TRYDAW

DANUSE

That's a bit too strong, Harry

LOCAL POL IS CROOKED

EDITOR

WHY THE EDITOR REJECTED THE ITALIC HEADLINE.

Now arrange the circled letters to form the surprise answer, as suggested by the above cartoon.

A: IT "⬜⬜⬜ " "⬜⬜⬜⬜⬜⬜⬜"

JUMBLE®

Unscramble these four Jumbles, one letter to each square, to form four ordinary words.

ATHEW

HALET

SINIST

SIGHAR

I must admit she has a wonderful voice

WHAT THE OPERA SINGER DID WHEN SHE TOOK THE OCEAN VOYAGE.

Now arrange the circled letters to form the surprise answer, as suggested by the above cartoon.

A: ☐☐☐ THE ☐☐☐☐ "☐☐☐☐"

JUMBLE®

Unscramble these four Jumbles, one letter to
each square, to form four ordinary words.

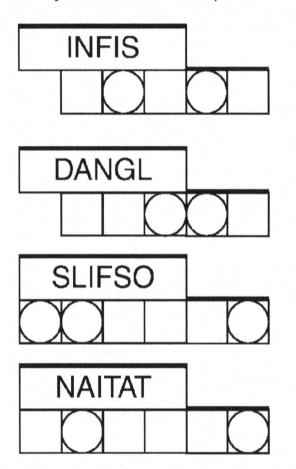

INFIS

DANGL

SLIFSO

NAITAT

$5 for a small
one, $10 for a
big one

I want
a big
one

WHAT DAD FACED
WHEN HE BOUGHT
A BALLOON.

Now arrange the circled letters to form the
surprise answer, as suggested by the above
cartoon.

Answer here:

JUMBLE®

Unscramble these four Jumbles, one letter to each square, to form four ordinary words.

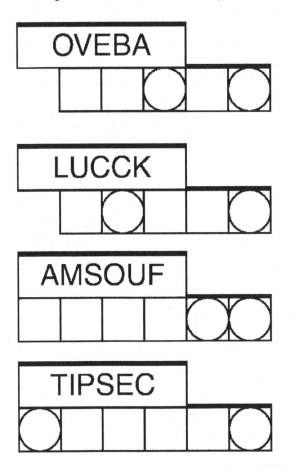

OVEBA

LUCCK

AMSOUF

TIPSEC

This 2 bedroom 2 bath is within your budget

A GOOD WAY TO SECURE HOUSING.

Now arrange the circled letters to form the surprise answer, as suggested by the above cartoon.

Answer here:

JUMBLE

Unscramble these four Jumbles, one letter to each square, to form four ordinary words.

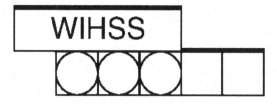

WIHSS

HURTT

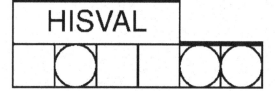

HISVAL

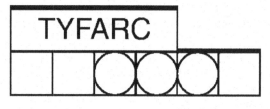

TYFARC

I can't believe —— it

WHAT THE JOCKEY SAID WHEN THE PERENNIAL ALSO-RAN WON THE RACE.

Now arrange the circled letters to form the surprise answer, as suggested by the above cartoon.

A: ⬡⬡⬡⬡⬡ ⬡⬡⬡ A "⬡⬡⬡⬡⬡"

JUMBLE®

Unscramble these four Jumbles, one letter to
each square, to form four ordinary words.

KLUSK

AMLET

WRAITE

DIPEEM

Follow their
path

We'll find
them

WHAT HAPPENED
WHEN THE THIEVES
RAN INTO THE
CORNFIELD?

Now arrange the circled letters to form the
surprise answer, as suggested by the above
cartoon.

A: THEY "⬜⬜⬜⬜ ⬜⬜⬜⬜⬜⬜⬜"

JUMBLE®

Unscramble these four Jumbles, one letter to
each square, to form four ordinary words.

LULET

HEWIG

CUBEKT

SESCUN

He's a
riot

WHEN THE SEWING
CLUB WATCHED THE
COMEDY SHOW,
THEY WERE---

Now arrange the circled letters to form the
surprise answer, as suggested by the above
cartoon.

Answer: IN " ◯◯◯◯◯◯◯◯ "

JUMBLE

Unscramble these four Jumbles, one letter to
each square, to form four ordinary words.

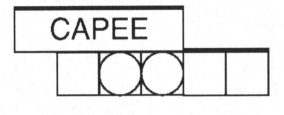

CAPEE

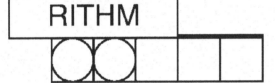

RITHM

YEMILT

KANTLE

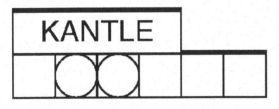

BON BON
CANDY CO.

He's worth
a fortune

He can
afford it

THE OWNER OF A
CANDY FACTORY
CAN DO THIS.

Now arrange the circled letters to form the
surprise answer, as suggested by the above
cartoon.

Answer: ⬡⬡⬡⬡ A " ⬡⬡⬡⬡ "

JUMBLE®

Unscramble these four Jumbles, one letter to each square, to form four ordinary words.

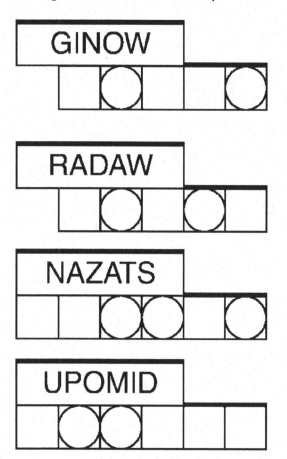

GINOW

RADAW

NAZATS

UPOMID

ALOON   DRY GOODS

That looks like Nellie

AN ARTIST AND A
HORSE CAN DO THIS.

Now arrange the circled letters to form the surprise answer, as suggested by the above cartoon.

Answer: " ◯◯◯◯ " A ◯◯◯◯◯◯

JUMBLE®

Unscramble these four Jumbles, one letter to
each square, to form four ordinary words.

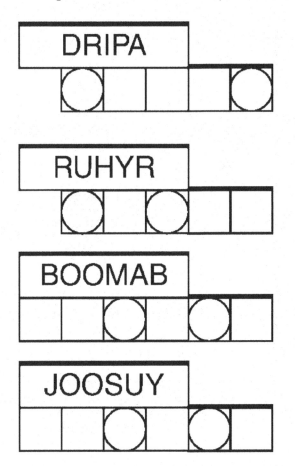

DRIPA

RUHYR

BOOMAB

JOOSUY

This machine is like
my last date—a lot
of hot air

WHAT THE NEIGH-
BORS SHARED IN
THE LAUNDRY ROOM.

Now arrange the circled letters to form the
surprise answer, as suggested by the above
cartoon.

Answer here: " ◯◯◯ " ◯◯◯◯◯◯

JUMBLE®

Unscramble these four Jumbles, one letter to
each square, to form four ordinary words.

VEYON

GLONI

PENXED

ZOLENZ

You've been
sitting there
for hours

Where are
my glasses?

WATCHING FOOT-
BALL ALL DAY CAN
AFFECT YOUR---

Now arrange the circled letters to form the
surprise answer, as suggested by the above
cartoon.

Print answer here: " ◯◯◯ " ◯◯◯◯

JUMBLE®

Unscramble these four Jumbles, one letter to each square, to form four ordinary words.

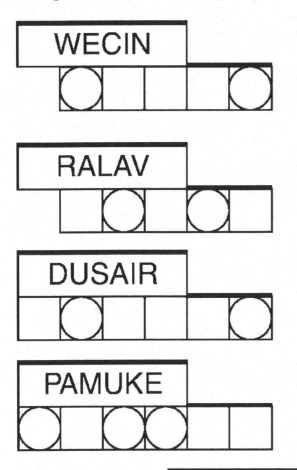

WECIN

RALAV

DUSAIR

PAMUKE

You get the top

Whatever you say

THE NEW SAILOR TOOK THE UPPER BUNK BECAUSE HE DIDN'T WANT TO----

Now arrange the circled letters to form the surprise answer, as suggested by the above cartoon.

Answer here:

JUMBLE®

Unscramble these four Jumbles, one letter to each square, to form four ordinary words.

BAINC

GLUBY

ELLAHT

SCEPHY

Therefore, I concluded that...

Your theory is enlightening

WHEN THE SCIEN- TISTS MET ON A CROSS-COUNTRY FLIGHT, THEY TALKED ON---

Now arrange the circled letters to form the surprise answer, as suggested by the above cartoon.

Answer: A ◯◯◯◯ " ◯◯◯◯◯ "

JUMBLE®

Unscramble these four Jumbles, one letter to each square, to form four ordinary words.

THACH

MEENY

RANTTY

MISOGE

What is it?

It's too big to be a snake

WHAT THE ITALIAN FISHERMAN SAID WHEN HE SNARED AN EEL IN HIS NET.

Now arrange the circled letters to form the surprise answer, as suggested by the above cartoon.

A: " ⬡⬡⬡⬡ ' ⬡ A ⬡⬡⬡⬡⬡ "

JUMBLE®

Unscramble these four Jumbles, one letter to each square, to form four ordinary words.

UGSIE

HYSIF

GAIWHE

HENBID

Everything is clean and new

I hope you like it, dear

WHAT THE EXCAVATOR ENJOYED WHEN HIS HOUSE WAS FINISHED?

Now arrange the circled letters to form the surprise answer, as suggested by the above cartoon.

Ans: ◯◯◯ ◯◯◯ " ◯◯◯◯ "

JUMBLE®

Unscramble these four Jumbles, one letter to each square, to form four ordinary words.

MERRA

GAPAN

OOTARR

CREEFI

Whooee! It's our best year ever

WHEN THE BUMPER CORN CROP LEFT THE FARMER GRIN- NING, IT WAS---

Now arrange the circled letters to form the surprise answer, as suggested by the above cartoon.

Ans: ☐☐☐☐ ☐☐☐ TO ☐☐☐

JUMBLE®

Unscramble these four Jumbles, one letter to
each square, to form four ordinary words.

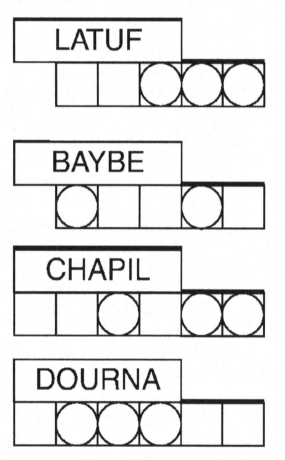

LATUF

BAYBE

CHAPIL

DOURNA

**WHERE'S
THE
RABBIT?**

WHEN THE TRICK
FAILED, THE MAGI-
CIAN WANTED TO----

Now arrange the circled letters to form the
surprise answer, as suggested by the above
cartoon.

A: ☐☐☐☐☐ HIS ☐☐☐☐☐ ☐☐☐

JUMBLE®

Unscramble these four Jumbles, one letter to
each square, to form four ordinary words.

EECIP

GIBEE

JINNOE

MERRIP

TO MANY, WHEN
MARRIAGE IS MEN-
TIONED, IT HAS A——

Now arrange the circled letters to form the
surprise answer, as suggested by the above
cartoon.

Answer: ⃝⃝⃝⃝ " ⃝⃝⃝⃝ " TO IT

JUMBLE®

Unscramble these four Jumbles, one letter to each square, to form four ordinary words.

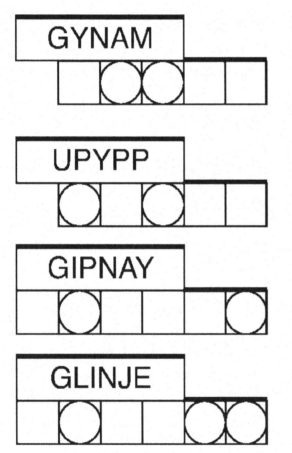

GYNAM

UPYPP

GIPNAY

GLINJE

We'll take this to the Supreme Court

He's so cute

WHEN HE LOST THE CASE, THE HANDSOME LAWYER WAS----

Now arrange the circled letters to form the surprise answer, as suggested by the above cartoon.

Answer: " ⬡⬡⬡⬡⬡⬡ ⬡⬡⬡ "

JUMBLE®

Unscramble these four Jumbles, one letter to each square, to form four ordinary words.

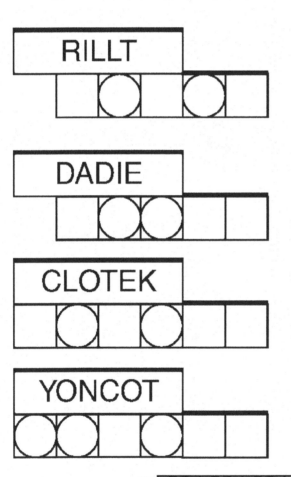

RILLT

DADIE

CLOTEK

YONCOT

Straight to the bathtub, mister

WHAT JUNIOR GOT WHEN HE CAME HOME FILTHY.

Now arrange the circled letters to form the surprise answer, as suggested by the above cartoon.

Answer: A " ⬡⬡⬡⬡⬡ " ⬡⬡⬡⬡

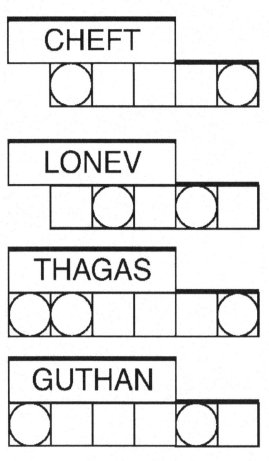

JUMBLE®

Unscramble these four Jumbles, one letter to each square, to form four ordinary words.

CHEFT

LONEV

THAGAS

GUTHAN

Make sure the line is tight and you have enough clothespins

WHAT SHE GOT WHEN SHE DRIED HER LAUNDRY OUTDOORS.

Now arrange the circled letters to form the surprise answer, as suggested by the above cartoon.

Ans: ☐☐☐ " ☐☐☐☐☐ " ☐☐ IT

JUMBLE®

Unscramble these four Jumbles, one letter to
each square, to form four ordinary words.

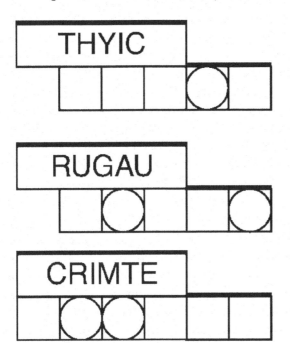

THYIC

RUGAU

CRIMTE

MANIAE

NYLONS

Hurry!
They're
50%
off

WHEN PANTYHOSE
WENT ON SALE,
THERE WAS A----

Now arrange the circled letters to form the
surprise answer, as suggested by the above
cartoon.

Answer here: "  " ON

JUMBLE®

Unscramble these four Jumbles, one letter to each square, to form four ordinary words.

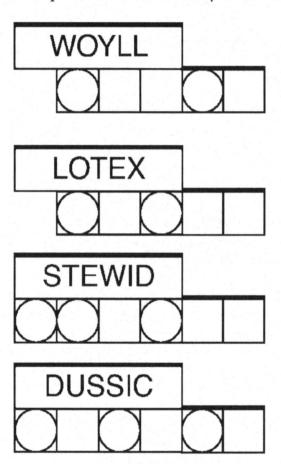

WOYLL

LOTEX

STEWID

DUSSIC

That's it. I made five spades

WHY THE NATTILY-DRESSED PLAYER WON THE BRIDGE HAND.

Now arrange the circled letters to form the surprise answer, as suggested by the above cartoon.

A: HE WAS " "

JUMBLE®

Unscramble these four Jumbles, one letter to each square, to form four ordinary words.

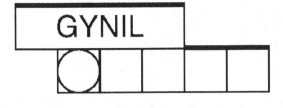

GYNIL

NUBOD

JALOCE

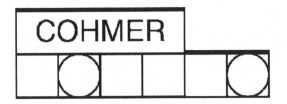

COHMER

He does everything

WHAT THE BOSS
DID IN THE
DOUGHNUT SHOP.

Now arrange the circled letters to form the surprise answer, as suggested by the above cartoon.

Answer here: THE "  "

JUMBLE®

Unscramble these four Jumbles, one letter to
each square, to form four ordinary words.

NYSOW

WRONC

KEENAW

ROHTAU

Be careful up there

WHAT MIGHT A TAXI
DRIVER USE TO
TRIM HIS TREES.

Now arrange the circled letters to form the
surprise answer, as suggested by the above
cartoon.

Answer here: A " ☐☐☐☐☐ " ☐☐☐

JUMBLE®

Unscramble these four Jumbles, one letter to
each square, to form four ordinary words.

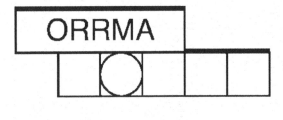

ORRMA

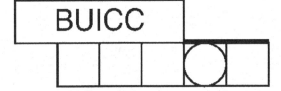

BUICC

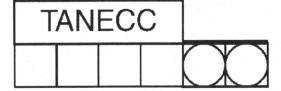

TANECC

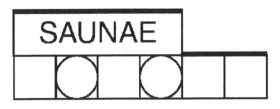

SAUNAE

Ouch! I think I pulled
a muscle in my back

EASY TO GET
WHEN ONE TRAINS.

Now arrange the circled letters to form the
surprise answer, as suggested by the above
cartoon.

Print answer here: A

JUMBLE®

Unscramble these four Jumbles, one letter to each square, to form four ordinary words.

EBILE

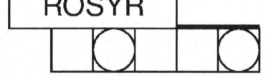

ROSYR

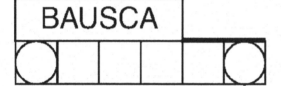

BAUSCA

BLUJEM

Do it right if you know what's good for you

That's it. I'm through

WHY THE MOBSTER'S TAILOR QUIT.

Now arrange the circled letters to form the surprise answer, as suggested by the above cartoon.

Ans: IT WAS A " ◯◯◯◯◯ " ◯◯◯

JUMBLE®

Unscramble these four Jumbles, one letter to
each square, to form four ordinary words.

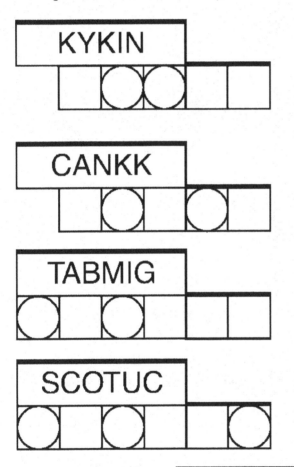

KYKIN

CANKK

TABMIG

SCOTUC

WHAT THE GIANT
WRESTLER WAS
INTERESTED IN WHEN
HE READ THE MENU.

Now arrange the circled letters to form the
surprise answer, as suggested by the above
cartoon.

Answer here:

JUMBLE

Unscramble these four Jumbles, one letter to each square, to form four ordinary words.

IRROG

YAHIR

HORBET

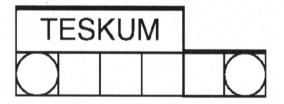
TESKUM

I'm never wrong

Ya gotta love him

SHE MARRIED THE KNOW-IT-ALL BECAUSE HE WAS---

Now arrange the circled letters to form the surprise answer, as suggested by the above cartoon.

Answer here:  ⬤⬤. " ⬤⬤⬤⬤⬤ "

JUMBLE®

Unscramble these four Jumbles, one letter to
each square, to form four ordinary words.

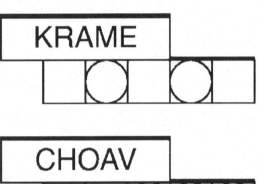

KRAME

CHOAV

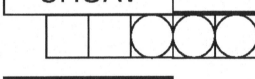

NALDIN

INGRYT

Turn on some music

This is a test. This is just a test

WHEN THE NUCLEAR
SCIENTIST TURNED
ON THE CAR
STEREO, HE WAS----

Now arrange the circled letters to form the
surprise answer, as suggested by the above
cartoon.

Ans: ⊙⊙⊙⊙⊙ ⊙⊙⊙⊙⊙⊙

JUMBLE®

Unscramble these four Jumbles, one letter to each square, to form four ordinary words.

BYMAL

TALAN

CAPUNK

AECIPE

Look! Isn't that...

OFTEN SPOTTED IN A FANCY RESTAURANT.

Now arrange the circled letters to form the surprise answer, as suggested by the above cartoon.

Print answer here: A ⃝⃝⃝⃝⃝⃝

JUMBLE

Unscramble these four Jumbles, one letter to each square, to form four ordinary words.

CULOT

RIBAN

TUNBOT

RESOOM

It'll be one and done

WHEN THE HEAVY-WEIGHT CHAMP WAS INTERVIEWED, IT WAS---

Now arrange the circled letters to form the surprise answer, as suggested by the above cartoon.

Answer: ☐☐☐☐☐ A ☐☐☐☐

JUMBLE®

Unscramble these four Jumbles, one letter to each square, to form four ordinary words.

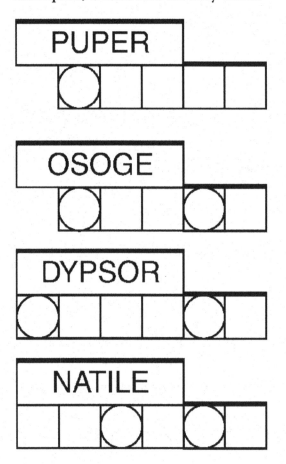

PUPER

OSOGE

DYPSOR

NATILE

Ugh! Men are such pigs

You should have seen the redhead

SOUNDS LIKE WHAT THEY DISCUSSED.

Now arrange the circled letters to form the surprise answer, as suggested by the above cartoon.

Print answer here:

JUMBLE

Unscramble these four Jumbles, one letter to each square, to form four ordinary words.

PRIPE

POZAT

GRENED

PROWED

What a surprise

We need a cold drink

WHY HIS PALS WERE LIKE ICE CUBES.

Now arrange the circled letters to form the surprise answer, as suggested by the above cartoon.

Ans: THEY " ⬡⬡⬡⬡⬡⬡⬡⬡ " ⬡⬡

JUMBLE®

Unscramble these four Jumbles, one letter to each square, to form four ordinary words.

MICHE

ZYZID

MAMBEL

AGANEM

How do we get out of here?

WHEN THE LITTLE INDIANS GOT LOST, THE CORN-FIELD BECAME A----

Now arrange the circled letters to form the surprise answer, as suggested by the above cartoon.

Answer here: ◯◯◯◯◯ ◯◯◯◯

JUMBLE

Unscramble these four Jumbles, one letter to each square, to form four ordinary words.

FROOL

JETEC

SIPHOL

DILFED

I had a wonderful time

Never again

WHAT HAPPENED WHEN SHE WENT OUT WITH THE AIR-CONDITIONING SALESMAN.

Now arrange the circled letters to form the surprise answer, as suggested by the above cartoon.

A: HE ⬡⬡⬡⬡ ⬡⬡⬡ " ⬡⬡⬡⬡⬡ "

JUMBLE®

Unscramble these four Jumbles, one letter to
each square, to form four ordinary words.

DAPAT

LEETA

STOFRY

REPHOG

Wow!

He's
mine

ALWAYS A POSSES-
SIVE INDICATION.

Now arrange the circled letters to form the
surprise answer, as suggested by the above
cartoon.

Ans: AN ☐☐☐☐☐☐☐☐☐☐☐

JUMBLE®

Unscramble these four Jumbles, one letter to
each square, to form four ordinary words.

ZEFOR

TYSUL

GLIJEG

CAPUTE

This warm
milk will
relax me

WHAT THE BOSS
DID WHEN HE WENT
TO BED FACING A
BIG DECISION.

Now arrange the circled letters to form the
surprise answer, as suggested by the above
cartoon.

Answer here: " ◯◯◯◯◯ " ON ◯◯

JUMBLE®

Unscramble these four Jumbles, one letter to each square, to form four ordinary words.

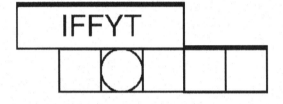

IFFYT

CELEX

NORACE

TINIVE

This is a big place, Homer

ANY WAY YOU LOOK AT IT, THIS PERTAINS TO A CITY.

Now arrange the circled letters to form the surprise answer, as suggested by the above cartoon.

Print answer here:

JUMBLE

Unscramble these four Jumbles, one letter to
each square, to form four ordinary words.

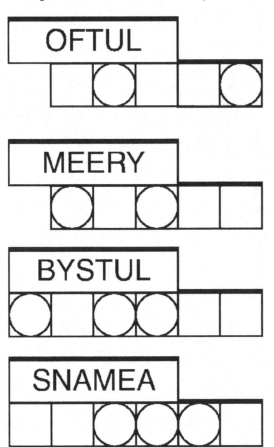

OFTUL

MEERY

BYSTUL

SNAMEA

Sidney is
always there
for me

WHAT THE HORSE
BREEDER CONSID-
ERED HER HUSBAND.

Now arrange the circled letters to form the
surprise answer, as suggested by the above
cartoon.

A: A " ⬡⬡⬡⬡⬡⬡ " ⬡⬡⬡⬡

JUMBLE®

Unscramble these four Jumbles, one letter to each square, to form four ordinary words.

OTAFO

YARIF

LADJIE

KNEBOC

Ahh! That hits the spot

WHAT DAD CONSIDERED THE ICY DRINK ON A HOT DAY.

Now arrange the circled letters to form the surprise answer, as suggested by the above cartoon.

Answer here: A

JUMBLE®

Unscramble these four Jumbles, one letter to each square, to form four ordinary words.

YAWLB

EMAHR

TREFER

PRAMCE

Wow! Look at all the women

A GOOD PLACE TO FIND A DATE.

Now arrange the circled letters to form the surprise answer, as suggested by the above cartoon.

Answer here: A ◯◯◯◯ ◯◯◯◯

JUMBLE®

Unscramble these four Jumbles, one letter to each square, to form four ordinary words.

JICUE

YONAN

GRAHNE

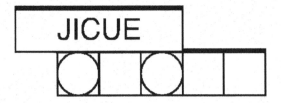

GRIFIN

...I'm gonna rock around the...

Stop! That's awful

Horace, QUIET!

WHAT MOM WILL DO WHEN THE KIDS OBJECT TO DAD'S SHOWER SINGING.

Now arrange the circled letters to form the surprise answer, as suggested by the above cartoon.

A:  THE "  "

JUMBLE®

Unscramble these four Jumbles, one letter to each square, to form four ordinary words.

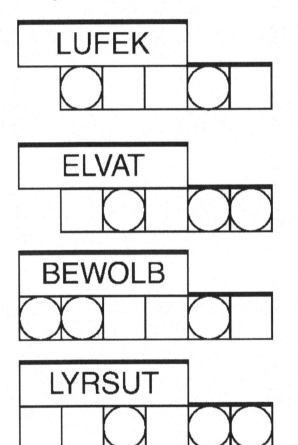

LUFEK

ELVAT

BEWOLB

LYRSUT

It is with great pleasure that I make your acquaintance

CAN BE HEARD AT A SNOOTY GARDEN PARTY.

Now arrange the circled letters to form the surprise answer, as suggested by the above cartoon.

A: "  "

JUMBLE®

Unscramble these four Jumbles, one letter to
each square, to form four ordinary words.

SKUYH

CAMKS

PAKRUM

COYPIL

When the wind
blows the...

ANOTHER NAME
FOR A LULLABY.

Now arrange the circled letters to form the
surprise answer, as suggested by the above
cartoon.

Answer: " ◯◯◯◯◯ " ◯◯◯◯◯◯

JUMBLE®

Unscramble these four Jumbles, one letter to each square, to form four ordinary words.

EVASU

DUILF

ODONEL

ABANCA

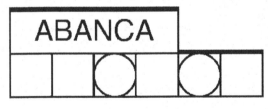

Must have used a slip knot

WHEN THE SAILOR DIDN'T TIE THE ROPE PROPERLY, IT WAS----

Now arrange the circled letters to form the surprise answer, as suggested by the above cartoon.

Ans: " ⬡⬡⬡⬡⬡ " TO ⬡⬡⬡⬡

JUMBLE®

Unscramble these four Jumbles, one letter to each square, to form four ordinary words.

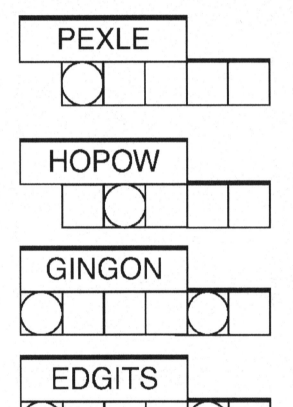

PEXLE

HOPOW

GINGON

EDGITS

You're doing a great job

Can I have the car tonight?

WHAT HAPPENED WHEN THE TEENAGER POLISHED DAD'S CAR.

Now arrange the circled letters to form the surprise answer, as suggested by the above cartoon.

Answer here: HE " ◯◯◯◯◯◯ "

JUMBLE

Unscramble these four Jumbles, one letter to each square, to form four ordinary words.

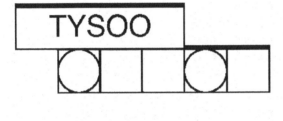

TYSOO

HYPON

SAYMUL

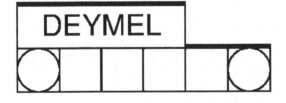

DEYMEL

Oh, my leg! Quick, bring me a bandage

Oh, you poor dear

WHAT THE DAIRY FARMER MILKED WHEN HE WAS KICKED BY OLD BETSY.

Now arrange the circled letters to form the surprise answer, as suggested by the above cartoon.

Print answer here:

JUMBLE®

Unscramble these four Jumbles, one letter to
each square, to form four ordinary words.

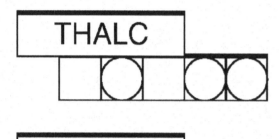

THALC

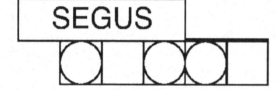

SEGUS

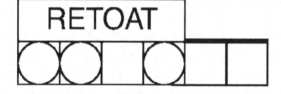

RETOAT

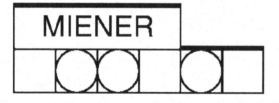

MIENER

Talk fast, it's expensive here

WHAT THE TOURISTS
PAID TO USE A
CELL PHONE IN
ITALY.

Now arrange the circled letters to form the
surprise answer, as suggested by the above
cartoon.

A: " ⬡⬡⬡⬡⬡ " ⬡⬡⬡⬡⬡⬡⬡

JUMBLE®

Unscramble these four Jumbles, one letter to
each square, to form four ordinary words.

BOJAN

MUIBE

GUEFER

MUCAUV

WHEN THE SMOKE-
BELCHING JALOPY
WENT BY, THE
PEDESTRIANS
WERE---

Now arrange the circled letters to form the
surprise answer, as suggested by the above
cartoon.

Print answer here: "⚪⚪⚪⚪⚪⚪"

85

JUMBLE®

Unscramble these four Jumbles, one letter to each square, to form four ordinary words.

INSEG

IDEPT

COBIXE

TEAGEN

Nothing to be afraid of

NO! NO!

THE BURLY WRES-
TLER REFUSED
ACUPUNCTURE
BECAUSE HE DIDN'T
WANT TO---

Now arrange the circled letters to form the surprise answer, as suggested by the above cartoon.

Answer: ⬤⬤⬤ " ⬤⬤⬤⬤⬤⬤ "

86

JUMBLE

Unscramble these four Jumbles, one letter to each square, to form four ordinary words.

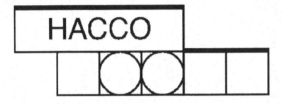

HACCO

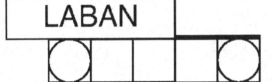

LABAN

DESMOT

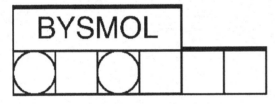

BYSMOL

FIREWORKS

It's like
this
every
year

THIS HAPPENS
BEFORE THE
FOURTH OF JULY.

Now arrange the circled letters to form the surprise answer, as suggested by the above cartoon.

Answer: ⬡⬡⬡⬡⬡ " ⬡⬡⬡⬡ "

JUMBLE®

Unscramble these four Jumbles, one letter to
each square, to form four ordinary words.

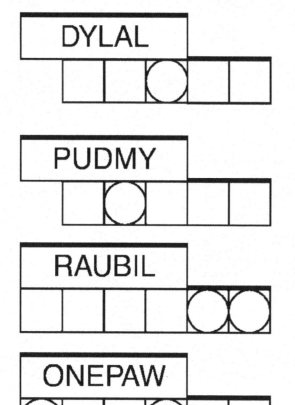

DYLAL

PUDMY

RAUBIL

ONEPAW

But I was going to play
golf and take a nap

Not today

WHERE HUBBY ENDED
UP ON HIS DAY OFF.

Now arrange the circled letters to form the
surprise answer, as suggested by the above
cartoon.

Print answer here:  THE

JUMBLE®

Unscramble these four Jumbles, one letter to each square, to form four ordinary words.

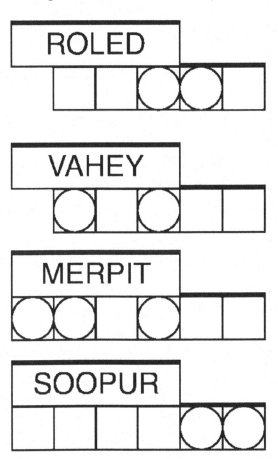

ROLED

VAHEY

MERPIT

SOOPUR

How would you use the eyeliner?

HOW THE COSMETICS STUDENT ARRIVED AT THE RIGHT ANSWER.

Now arrange the circled letters to form the surprise answer, as suggested by the above cartoon.

Ans: ◯◯◯ " ◯◯◯◯◯ IT ◯◯ "

JUMBLE®

Unscramble these four Jumbles, one letter to
each square, to form four ordinary words.

LIDAY

TIELE

SIMFLY

DEFLAB

There's a lot
of car chases

NOW
PLAYING

Any
romance?

WHAT THE MOVIE
ABOUT THE
MOONSHINER
TURNED INTO.

Now arrange the circled letters to form the
surprise answer, as suggested by the above
cartoon.

Answer: A "⬚⬚⬚⬚⬚⬚" ⬚⬚⬚⬚

JUMBLE®

Unscramble these four Jumbles, one letter to each square, to form four ordinary words.

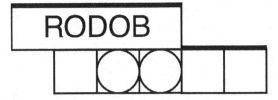

RODOB

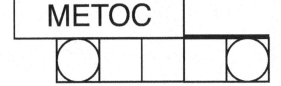

METOC

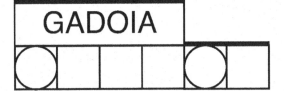

GADOIA

FISHMA

The wheels were a good idea

THE KIDS TURNED THE ABANDONED RECLINER INTO A---

Now arrange the circled letters to form the surprise answer, as suggested by the above cartoon.

Answer: " ⬚⬚⬚⬚⬚ - ⬚⬚⬚ "

JUMBLE®

Unscramble these four Jumbles, one letter to
each square, to form four ordinary words.

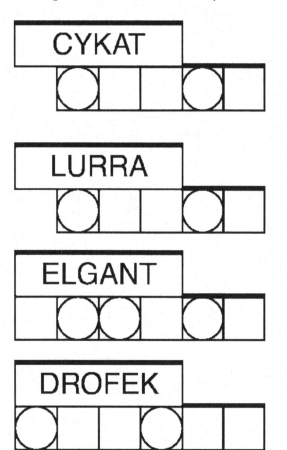

CYKAT

LURRA

ELGANT

DROFEK

First the mustard, then the
relish, then the onion...

WHAT THE HOT
DOG VENDOR GAVE
HIS NEW HELPER.

Now arrange the circled letters to form the
surprise answer, as suggested by the above
cartoon.

Answer: "⬭⬭⬭⬭⬭" ⬭⬭⬭⬭

JUMBLE®

Unscramble these four Jumbles, one letter to each square, to form four ordinary words.

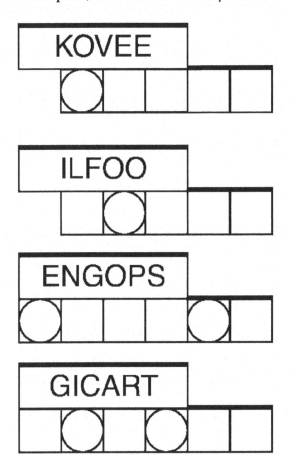

KOVEE

ILFOO

ENGOPS

GICART

The view is breathtaking

HOW THE HIKERS DESCRIBED THE CAMPSITE OVER-LOOKING THE CANYONS.

Now arrange the circled letters to form the surprise answer, as suggested by the above cartoon.

Print answer here: "  "

93

JUMBLE

Unscramble these four Jumbles, one letter to
each square, to form four ordinary words.

YUINT

BROOT

YATGIE

ENBARN

It costs
$50 an
hour

Where do I
put the key?

STUDENT
DRIVER

WHAT HE PAID
WHEN HE WENT TO
DRIVING SCHOOL.

Now arrange the circled letters to form the
surprise answer, as suggested by the above
cartoon.

Answer here: ◯◯◯◯◯◯◯◯◯◯

JUMBLE

Unscramble these four Jumbles, one letter to each square, to form four ordinary words.

GREME

TINEW

HESTEE

MACPIT

Too much food, too little exercise

DEVELOPING A POT BELLY OVER THE YEARS IS A---

Now arrange the circled letters to form the surprise answer, as suggested by the above cartoon.

Ans: " ⬡⬡⬡⬡⬡ " OF ⬡⬡⬡⬡

JUMBLE®

Unscramble these four Jumbles, one letter to each square, to form four ordinary words.

FROYE

TIBEF

HOTFRY

REEKUB

Whew!

HOW THE TENDER-FOOT FELT WHEN HE FELL FROM THE HORSE AFTER THE LONG RIDE.

Now arrange the circled letters to form the surprise answer, as suggested by the above cartoon.

Answer: ⬡⬡⬡⬡⬡⬡ " ⬡⬡⬡ "

JUMBLE®

Unscramble these four Jumbles, one letter to each square, to form four ordinary words.

PLUIP

SYRTT

GLUNJE

PIMNED

Georgie and Rover are inseparable

WHERE THE DOG SLEPT WHEN THE FAMILY WENT CAMPING.

Now arrange the circled letters to form the surprise answer, as suggested by the above cartoon.

Answer here: IN THE " ◯◯◯ " ◯◯◯◯

97

JUMBLE

Unscramble these four Jumbles, one letter to each square, to form four ordinary words.

ROSTN

RINBY

REYYAL

WARTOD

He'll sleep it off

9-20

WHAT HAPPENED WHEN THE COWBOY CAUSED TROUBLE AT THE SALOON.

Now arrange the circled letters to form the surprise answer, as suggested by the above cartoon.

Ans: HE ⬡⬡⬡ " ⬡⬡⬡⬡⬡⬡ "

JUMBLE®

Unscramble these four Jumbles, one letter to each square, to form four ordinary words.

KROOB

GILEA

BLONGO

SAYQUE

Good idea. Sales are way up

Two beers

DISCOUNTED HAPPY HOUR DRINKS CAN RESULT IN----

Now arrange the circled letters to form the surprise answer, as suggested by the above cartoon.

Answer here: " ◯◯◯ - ◯◯◯◯◯ "

JUMBLE®

Unscramble these four Jumbles, one letter to each square, to form four ordinary words.

GORCA

CATHY

WALLUF

BORTED

Stay together when you harmonize

WHAT THE COUPLE LEARNED WHEN THEY TOOK SINGING LESSONS.

Now arrange the circled letters to form the surprise answer, as suggested by the above cartoon.

Answer here: ◯◯◯ TO "◯◯◯◯"

JUMBLE®

Unscramble these four Jumbles, one letter to each square, to form four ordinary words.

SENWY

KARCC

LAHRDY

CROSCH

Now I can string up the hammock

POLICE

WHY THE CON MAN PLANTED TREES IN HIS BACK YARD.

Now arrange the circled letters to form the surprise answer, as suggested by the above cartoon.

Ans: IT WAS " ☐☐☐☐☐ " ☐☐☐☐

JUMBLE®

Unscramble these four Jumbles, one letter to
each square, to form four ordinary words.

KYMIL

LAHCK

PANMEC

DOUBEY

That's it! You
lose $20

WHEN HE LOST
THE CHESS GAME,
HE---

Now arrange the circled letters to form the
surprise answer, as suggested by the above
cartoon.

Ans: ☐☐☐☐ BY " ☐☐☐☐☐ "

JUMBLE®

Unscramble these four Jumbles, one letter to
each square, to form four ordinary words.

GEDEH

CUIMS

FLYJOU

CAPALA

10% discount
if you pay now

LOW
MONTHLY
RATES

HOW HE PAID FOR
THE FREEZER.

Now arrange the circled letters to form the
surprise answer, as suggested by the above
cartoon.

Answer here: " ⬡⬡⬡⬡ " ⬡⬡⬡⬡

JUMBLE®

Unscramble these four Jumbles, one letter to
each square, to form four ordinary words.

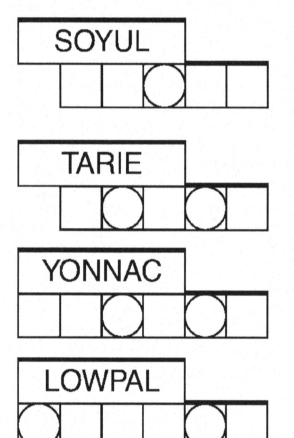

SOYUL

TARIE

YONNAC

LOWPAL

I'm tired of changing and
my feet are killing me

HOW THE MODEL
FELT AFTER THE
LONG FASHION
SHOW.

Now arrange the circled letters to form the
surprise answer, as suggested by the above
cartoon.

Print answer here: "  "

104

JUMBLE

Unscramble these four Jumbles, one letter to
each square, to form four ordinary words.

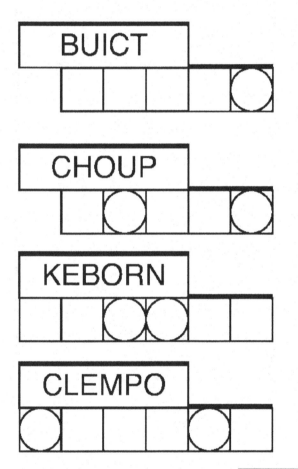

BUICT

CHOUP

KEBORN

CLEMPO

I ordered
it rare

WHEN THE DINER
SAID, "WELL DONE,"
HE WASN'T PRAISING——

Now arrange the circled letters to form the
surprise answer, as suggested by the above
cartoon.

Print answer here:

JUMBLE®

Unscramble these four Jumbles, one letter to
each square, to form four ordinary words.

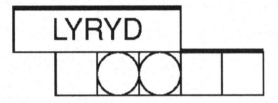

LYRYD

TABEA

MALEYS

TAUNER

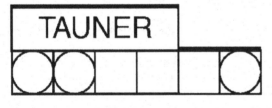

I would
never buy
that

I can't
imagine

WHEN SHE MOD-
ELED THE SKIMPY
BEACHWEAR, SHE
WAS———

Now arrange the circled letters to form the
surprise answer, as suggested by the above
cartoon.

Ans: "⬡⬡⬡⬡⬡⬡⬡" ⬡⬡⬡⬡

JUMBLE®

Unscramble these four Jumbles, one letter to
each square, to form four ordinary words.

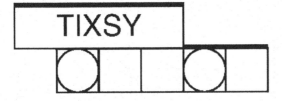

TIXSY

ZARUE

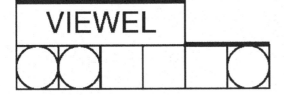

VIEWEL

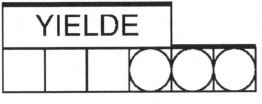

YIELDE

You have the snob
appeal we need

THE SHARP
DRESSER GOT THE
JOB AT THE MEN'S
STORE BECAUSE HE
WAS---

Now arrange the circled letters to form the
surprise answer, as suggested by the above
cartoon.

A: ◯◯◯◯ - "◯◯◯◯◯◯◯"

JUMBLE®

Unscramble these four Jumbles, one letter to each square, to form four ordinary words.

NOLFE

NAGIT

GAROUC

DEKOOH

There goes my curly hair

WHY THE PRISONER VISITED THE BARBER.

Now arrange the circled letters to form the surprise answer, as suggested by the above cartoon.

A: TO "⟨ ⟩"

JUMBLE®

Unscramble these four Jumbles, one letter to each square, to form four ordinary words.

THILG

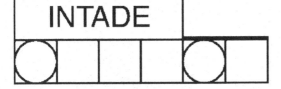

RAMOA

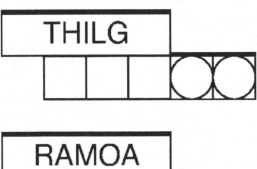

INTADE

TAKEGS

You didn't learn your tables. Extra — homework tonight

WHAT THE PUPILS EXPERIENCED WHEN THEY FAILED THE MULTIPLICATION TEST.

Now arrange the circled letters to form the surprise answer, as suggested by the above cartoon.

Answer: ◯◯◯◯ " ◯◯◯◯◯◯ "

JUMBLE®

Unscramble these four Jumbles, one letter to each square, to form four ordinary words.

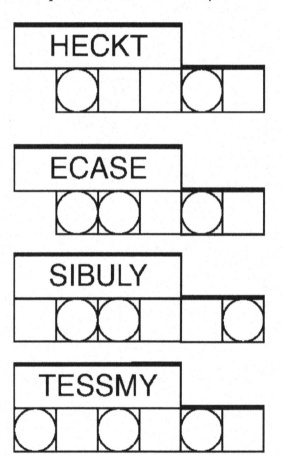

HECKT

ECASE

SIBULY

TESSMY

This is my best friend

He's always practicing

WHAT THE CON-
CERT PIANIST
CONSIDERED
HIS PIANO.

Now arrange the circled letters to form the surprise answer, as suggested by the above cartoon.

A: HIS " ☐☐☐☐ " TO ☐☐☐☐☐☐☐

JUMBLE®

Unscramble these four Jumbles, one letter to
each square, to form four ordinary words.

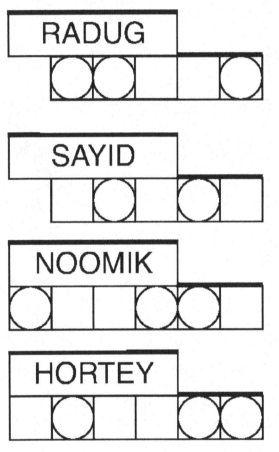

RADUG

SAYID

NOOMIK

HORTEY

The fault is right here

I don't
believe
you're
right

WHEN THE
RESEARCHER
COMPLETED HIS
EARTHQUAKE
STUDY, HE WAS----

Now arrange the circled letters to form the
surprise answer, as suggested by the above
cartoon.

A: ON " ⬡⬡⬡⬡⬡ " ⬡⬡⬡⬡⬡⬡

JUMBLE®

Unscramble these four Jumbles, one letter to each square, to form four ordinary words.

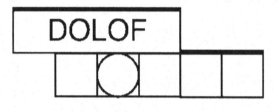

DOLOF

CAPEN

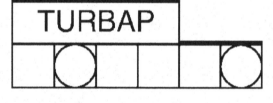

TURBAP

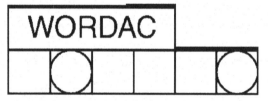

WORDAC

I'm outta here

CLICK

IRS IRS

WHAT THE TAX-
DODGING LOCK-
SMITH DID WHEN
THE IRS ARRIVED.

Now arrange the circled letters to form the
surprise answer, as suggested by the above
cartoon.

Print answer here: HE "  "

JUMBLE®

Unscramble these four Jumbles, one letter to
each square, to form four ordinary words.

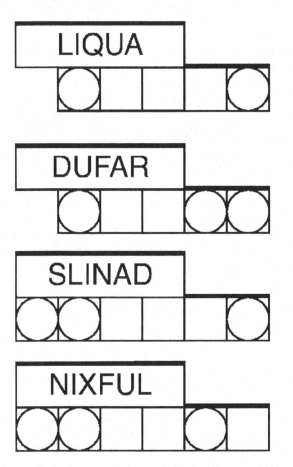

LIQUA

DUFAR

SLINAD

NIXFUL

A drink for everyone!

He just won the lottery

HE BOUGHT A
ROUND FOR THE
HOUSE BECAUSE
HE HAD----

Now arrange the circled letters to form the
surprise answer, as suggested by the above
cartoon.

A: " ⎵⎵⎵⎵⎵⎵⎵ " ⎵⎵⎵⎵⎵

JUMBLE®

Unscramble these four Jumbles, one letter to each square, to form four ordinary words.

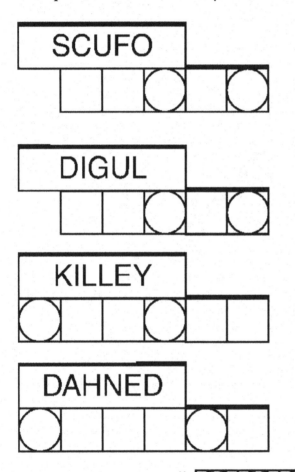

SCUFO

DIGUL

KILLEY

DAHNED

That doesn't look like me!

But I'm only on my third lesson

WHEN THE MOGUL PAID FOR HIS BUST, HE WAS----

Now arrange the circled letters to form the surprise answer, as suggested by the above cartoon.

Answer here: " ◯◯◯◯◯◯◯◯◯ "

JUMBLE®

Unscramble these four Jumbles, one letter to
each square, to form four ordinary words.

RAPPE

KEVAN

PLOMYC

REDOAF

Four
clubs

I think he's
bluffing

A GOOD THING TO
HAVE WHEN PLAYING
A BRIDGE HAND.

Now arrange the circled letters to form the
surprise answer, as suggested by the above
cartoon.

Answer: A "⬡⬡⬡⬡⬡" ⬡⬡⬡⬡

JUMBLE®

Unscramble these four Jumbles, one letter to each square, to form four ordinary words.

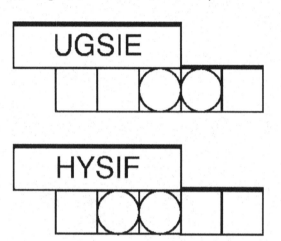

UGSIE

HYSIF

GAIWHE

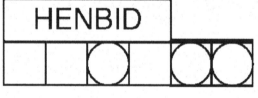

HENBID

Everything is clean and new

I hope you like it, dear

WHAT THE EXCAVATOR ENJOYED WHEN HIS HOUSE WAS FINISHED?

Now arrange the circled letters to form the surprise answer, as suggested by the above cartoon.

Ans: ◯◯◯◯ ◯◯◯ " ◯◯◯◯◯ "

JUMBLE®

Unscramble these four Jumbles, one letter to
each square, to form four ordinary words.

CILLA

OMACE

MELTIG

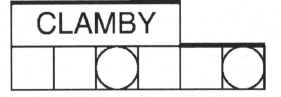

CLAMBY

Hmm!
This one
smells
good

WHAT THE POST-
MAN DELIVERED TO
THE BACHELOR.

Now arrange the circled letters to form the
surprise answer, as suggested by the above
cartoon.

Answer here:

117

JUMBLE®

Unscramble these four Jumbles, one letter to each square, to form four ordinary words.

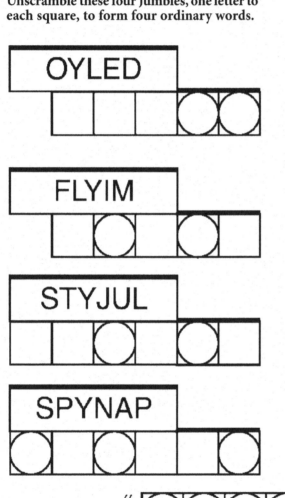

OYLED

FLYIM

STYJUL

SPYNAP

Drat, I missed

BANG!

HOW THE HUNTER STALKED HIS PREY WHEN HE LOST HIS RIFLE SCOPE.

Now arrange the circled letters to form the surprise answer, as suggested by the above cartoon.

Answer: " ◯◯◯◯◯◯◯◯◯ "

JUMBLE

Unscramble these four Jumbles, one letter to each square, to form four ordinary words.

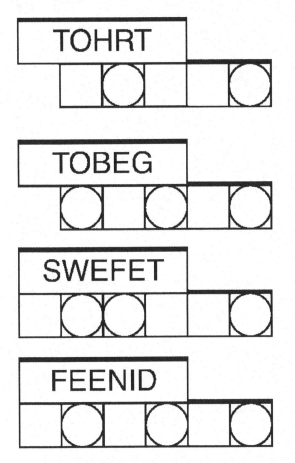

TOHRT

TOBEG

SWEFET

FEENID

I didn't lose a pound. This plan isn't working

WHAT THE DIETER LOOKED FOR WHEN HE GOT ON THE SCALE.

Now arrange the circled letters to form the surprise answer, as suggested by the above cartoon.

A: A ⬡⬡⬡⬡⬡⬡ " ⬡⬡⬡⬡⬡ "

JUMBLE®

Unscramble these four Jumbles, one letter to each square, to form four ordinary words.

ROJEK

RUMON

LATHEC

MEETOL

There are so many choices

WHAT THE SERVER ACCESSED ON HIS COMPUTER.

Now arrange the circled letters to form the surprise answer, as suggested by the above cartoon.

Print answer here: ☐☐☐ " ☐☐☐☐ "

JUMBLE®

Unscramble these four Jumbles, one letter to each square, to form four ordinary words.

WONNK

DYSAN

TORNGS

OTTYNK

Get up

I will not

WHAT HE DID WHILE SITTING.

Now arrange the circled letters to form the surprise answer, as suggested by the above cartoon.

Answer: ⬡⬡⬡⬡ A " ⬡⬡⬡⬡⬡ "

121

JUMBLE.

Unscramble these four Jumbles, one letter to
each square, to form four ordinary words.

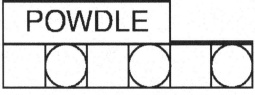

TIFED

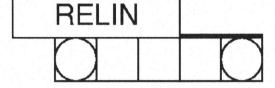

RELIN

VIKONE

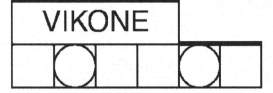

POWDLE

Just a cavity.
This won't
take long

WHY HE WASN'T
AFRAID TO GO TO
THE DENTIST.

Now arrange the circled letters to form the
surprise answer, as suggested by the above
cartoon.

A: HE ⬡⬡⬡⬡ THE " ⬡⬡⬡⬡⬡ "

JUMBLE®

Unscramble these four Jumbles, one letter to each square, to form four ordinary words.

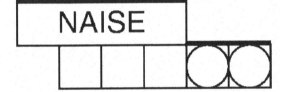
ROGOM

NAISE

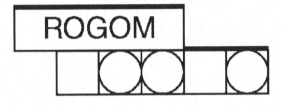
LEFZIZ

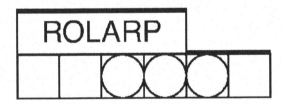
ROLARP

I made a nice profit

FOR SALE
SOLD

A GOOD WAY TO BETTER YOUR LOT.

Now arrange the circled letters to form the surprise answer, as suggested by the above cartoon.

A: ⬡⬡⬡⬡⬡ IT ⬡⬡⬡ ⬡⬡⬡⬡

JUMBLE®

Unscramble these four Jumbles, one letter to
each square, to form four ordinary words.

ZALEH

VEVER

RAWHOR

SHRAID

There goes my permanent

WHAT THE GIRL
GOT WHEN THEY
FROLICKED IN
THE OCEAN.

Now arrange the circled letters to form the
surprise answer, as suggested by the above
cartoon.

A: " ⬡⬡⬡⬡⬡⬡ " IN ⬡⬡⬡ ⬡⬡⬡⬡

JUMBLE®

Unscramble these four Jumbles, one letter to each square, to form four ordinary words.

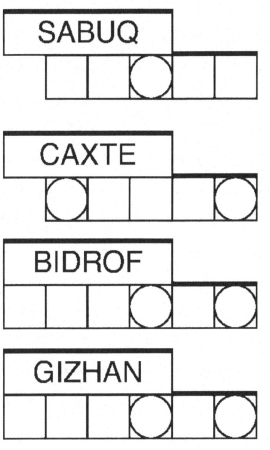

SABUQ

CAXTE

BIDROF

GIZHAN

Not enough income again

THE COUPLE WAS ALWAYS IN DEBT BECAUSE THEY COULDN'T---

Now arrange the circled letters to form the surprise answer, as suggested by the above cartoon.

Answer here: " ◯◯◯◯◯ ◯◯ "

JUMBLE®

Unscramble these four Jumbles, one letter to
each square, to form four ordinary words.

YOOBT

FRASC

BINNGE

TICCAR

The balance sheet
looks good, but I'm
worried about...

WHEN THE
FINANCIER STUDIED
THE MERGER, HE
FOUND IT---

Now arrange the circled letters to form the
surprise answer, as suggested by the above
cartoon.

Answer: " ⬡⬡⬡⬡⬡⬡⬡⬡⬡⬡ "

JUMBLE

Unscramble these four Jumbles, one letter to each square, to form four ordinary words.

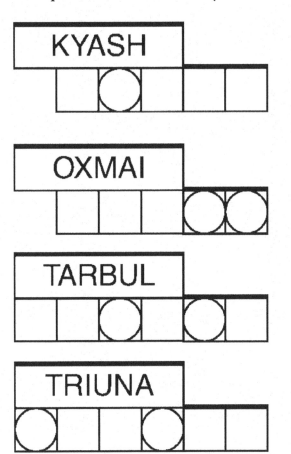

KYASH

OXMAI

TARBUL

TRIUNA

This is quite an honor

He deserves it

WHEN HE WAS NAMED "WATCH-MAKER OF THE YEAR," HE BECAME THE----

Now arrange the circled letters to form the surprise answer, as suggested by the above cartoon.

Answer here:  OF THE "  "

JUMBLE®

Unscramble these four Jumbles, one letter to
each square, to form four ordinary words.

FEYHT

DAJED

STAFLE

RISMEY

THE MAROONED
THEATERGOER
FINALLY GOT A----

Now arrange the circled letters to form the
surprise answer, as suggested by the above
cartoon.

A: ⬡⬡⬡⬡ ON ⬡⬡⬡ ⬡⬡⬡⬡

JUMBLE®

Unscramble these four Jumbles, one letter to each square, to form four ordinary words.

AMMAD

HARCI

DENAIG

DEGEWD

I'm next

No, I am

I need this shortened

HOW THE OVER-WORKED SEAM-STRESS FELT.

Now arrange the circled letters to form the surprise answer, as suggested by the above cartoon.

Answer here: " ⬚⬚⬚⬚⬚⬚ " ⬚⬚

He ran a red light

JUMBLE®

Unscramble these four Jumbles, one letter to each square, to form four ordinary words.

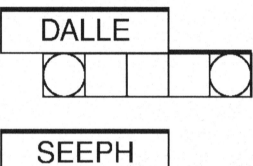

DALLE

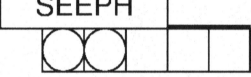

SEEPH

DESAUB

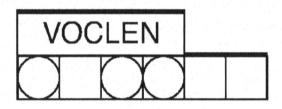

VOCLEN

WHAT THE BARBER EXPERIENCED ON HIS WAY TO WORK.

Now arrange the circled letters to form the surprise answer, as suggested by the above cartoon.

A: A ⬡⬡⬡⬡⬡ " ⬡⬡⬡⬡⬡ "

JUMBLE®

Unscramble these four Jumbles, one letter to each square, to form four ordinary words.

PUBYM

AXMMI

NERUNG

TRUVIE

WHAT THE JUDGE CONSIDERED THE HIGH-PROFILE CASE.

Now arrange the circled letters to form the surprise answer, as suggested by the above cartoon.

Print answer here: " ◯◯◯◯◯◯ "

JUMBLE®

Unscramble these four Jumbles, one letter to
each square, to form four ordinary words.

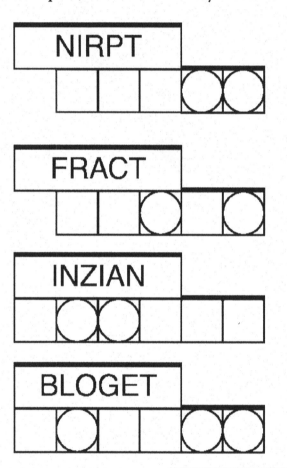

NIRPT

FRACT

INZIAN

BLOGET

WHAT THE SIDEWALK
ARTIST DREW.

Now arrange the circled letters to form the
surprise answer, as suggested by the above
cartoon.

Answer here: ⬡⬡⬡⬡⬡⬡⬡⬡⬡

JUMBLE

Unscramble these four Jumbles, one letter to each square, to form four ordinary words.

DUJEG

YOHBB

DEAGAN

FRYLUR

You do the towels

WHAT THE POKER PLAYER DID WHEN HE HELPED WITH THE LAUNDRY.

Now arrange the circled letters to form the surprise answer, as suggested by the above cartoon.

Answer here: ⬡⬡ " ⬡⬡⬡⬡⬡⬡ "

JUMBLE®

Unscramble these four Jumbles, one letter to each square, to form four ordinary words.

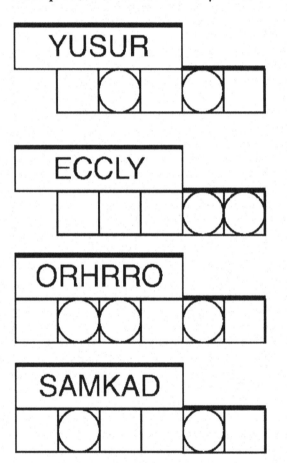

YUSUR

ECCLY

ORHRRO

SAMKAD

That's the fourth time they beat us

FINISH LINE

WHEN HE LOST THE HOT AIR BALLOON RACE, HE BECAME A----

Now arrange the circled letters to form the surprise answer, as suggested by the above cartoon.

Answer: " ⭕⭕⭕⭕ " ⭕⭕⭕⭕⭕

134

JUMBLE®

Unscramble these four Jumbles, one letter to
each square, to form four ordinary words.

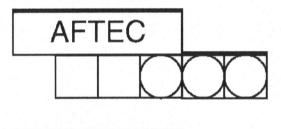

AFTEC

WOREC

TOOSHE

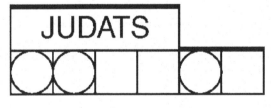

JUDATS

On the house?

Not a chance,
but try this

WHAT HAPPENED TO
THE RUMOR OF
FREE DRINKS?

Now arrange the circled letters to form the
surprise answer, as suggested by the above
cartoon.

A: IT ◯◯◯◯ "◯◯◯◯◯◯◯◯◯◯"

JUMBLE®

Unscramble these four Jumbles, one letter to each square, to form four ordinary words.

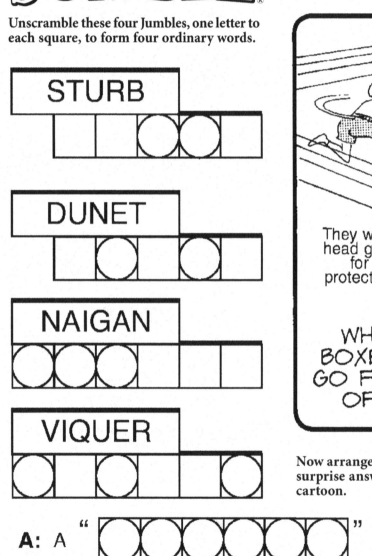

STURB

DUNET

NAIGAN

VIQUER

They wear head gear for protection

WHAT THE GYM BOXERS USED TO GO FOR A COUPLE OF "ROUNDS."

Now arrange the circled letters to form the surprise answer, as suggested by the above cartoon.

A: A "◯◯◯◯◯◯" ◯◯◯◯

JUMBLE®

Unscramble these four Jumbles, one letter to
each square, to form four ordinary words.

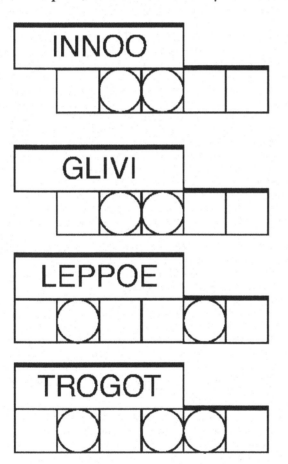

INNOO

GLIVI

LEPPOE

TROGOT

I hope I can find them
good homes

10-22

WHEN HIS DOG
HAD PUPPIES, THE
STREET CLEANER
SAID IT WAS----

Now arrange the circled letters to form the
surprise answer, as suggested by the above
cartoon.

Answer: " ⬡⬡⬡⬡⬡⬡⬡⬡⬡ "

JUMBLE

Unscramble these four Jumbles, one letter to
each square, to form four ordinary words.

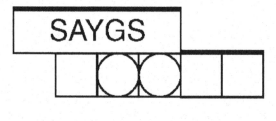

SAYGS

WHART

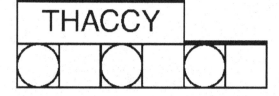

THACCY

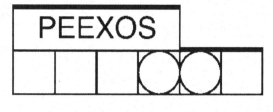

PEEXOS

I forgot my wallet

ALTHOUGH THE
LANKY BASKETBALL
PLAYER WAS LONG
ON TALENT, HE
WAS——

Now arrange the circled letters to form the
surprise answer, as suggested by the above
cartoon.

Ans: " ☐☐☐☐☐ " ON ☐☐☐☐

JUMBLE®

Unscramble these four Jumbles, one letter to
each square, to form four ordinary words.

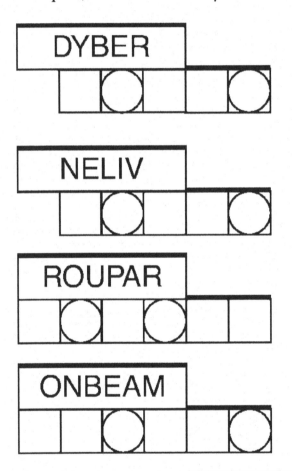

DYBER

NELIV

ROUPAR

ONBEAM

One-two-three.
You're out

He gets
the belt

WHAT THE PRO
WRESTLER GOT
WHEN HE WON
THE MATCH.

Now arrange the circled letters to form the
surprise answer, as suggested by the above
cartoon.

Answer here: " ◯◯◯ " ◯◯◯◯◯

JUMBLE

Unscramble these four Jumbles, one letter to each square, to form four ordinary words.

LORBI

SYSMO

SWILEY

GANTEM

Nice job. you pass

HOW HE PER-FORMED IN THE LIFEGUARD TEST.

Now arrange the circled letters to form the surprise answer, as suggested by the above cartoon.

Ans: " ◯◯◯◯◯◯◯◯◯◯ "

140

JUMBLE

Unscramble these four Jumbles, one letter to each square, to form four ordinary words.

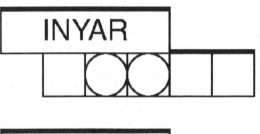

INYAR

TECOT

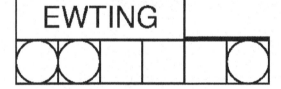

EWTING

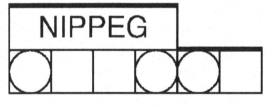

NIPPEG

Run to the car

What about the food?

WHEN RAIN HITS A PICNIC, IT CAN----

Now arrange the circled letters to form the surprise answer, as suggested by the above cartoon.

A: "◯◯◯" AN ◯◯◯◯◯◯◯◯◯

JUMBLE®

Unscramble these four Jumbles, one letter to
each square, to form four ordinary words.

VERPO

LYDAM

ENTELG

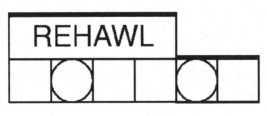

REHAWL

I'm going to Mother's!
GOOD-BYE!

WHEN HIS WIFE
STORMED OUT
AFTER THEIR ARGU-
MENT, SHE TOOK----

Now arrange the circled letters to form the
surprise answer, as suggested by the above
cartoon.

Answer here:

JUMBLE®

Unscramble these four Jumbles, one letter to each square, to form four ordinary words.

ABNIS

CLOIG

WYLLOH

SPOMIE

C'mon, Pat. You're falling behind

FINISH LINE

WHERE TO FIND RUNNERS-UP NO MATTER WHO WINS THE RACE.

Now arrange the circled letters to form the surprise answer, as suggested by the above cartoon.

A: ◯◯ A ◯◯◯◯◯ ◯◯◯◯◯◯

JUMBLE®

Unscramble these four Jumbles, one letter to each square, to form four ordinary words.

NAPCI

TALNS

YERSEG

DIZAWR

This is harder than I thought

AT THE END OF THE DAY, THE PLUMBER'S NEW HELPER SAID THE WORK WAS---

Now arrange the circled letters to form the surprise answer, as suggested by the above cartoon.

Answer here: " ◯◯◯◯◯◯◯◯ "

144

JUMBLE

Unscramble these four Jumbles, one letter to
each square, to form four ordinary words.

ENVOM

TANEC

SERJEY

PRELIF

For me?
What's in
here, darling?

WHAT A "PRESENT"
CAN BE.

Now arrange the circled letters to form the
surprise answer, as suggested by the above
cartoon.

Print answer here: A

JUMBLE®

Unscramble these four Jumbles, one letter to each square, to form four ordinary words.

GUDOH

GANGI

CLUMES

COMINE

Taste this

It's his hobby ___

He looks it

TO SOME, AN INTEREST IN FOOD CAN BE----

Now arrange the circled letters to form the surprise answer, as suggested by the above cartoon.

Answer: " ◯◯◯◯◯◯◯◯◯◯ "

JUMBLE®

Unscramble these four Jumbles, one letter to each square, to form four ordinary words.

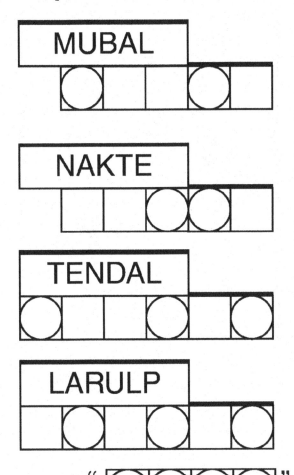

MUBAL

NAKTE

TENDAL

LARULP

It'll be dry tomorrow if it doesn't rain

Really?

WHAT THE SHARP DRESSER TURNED OUT TO BE.

Now arrange the circled letters to form the surprise answer, as suggested by the above cartoon.

A: A " ⬭⬭⬭⬭ " ⬭⬭⬭⬭⬭⬭

147

JUMBLE®

Unscramble these four Jumbles, one letter to
each square, to form four ordinary words.

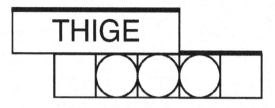

THIGE

MAGDO

MESHEC

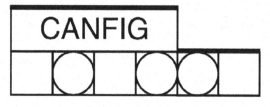

CANFIG

O.K.
you win.
I did it

WHAT THE COPS
DID WHEN THEY
QUESTIONED THE
CROONER.

Now arrange the circled letters to form the
surprise answer, as suggested by the above
cartoon.

A:

JUMBLE®

Unscramble these four Jumbles, one letter to each square, to form four ordinary words.

YOCEV

ADUCT

NOAWHY

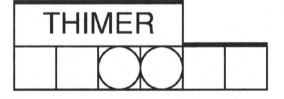

THIMER

In recognition of 40 years of meritorious service...

WHEN THE RETIREE WAS HONORED WITH A GOLD WATCH, HE BECAME THE---

Now arrange the circled letters to form the surprise answer, as suggested by the above cartoon.

Answer here:

 OF THE

JUMBLE®

Unscramble these four Jumbles, one letter to each square, to form four ordinary words.

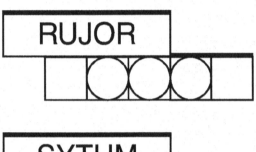

RUJOR

SYTUM

CUCHIP

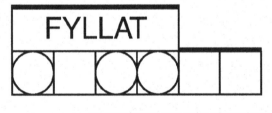

FYLLAT

He's dressed to kill

I hope — not

WHAT THE KNIFE THROWER WORE ON STAGE.

Now arrange the circled letters to form the surprise answer, as suggested by the above cartoon.

A: A "⬭⬭⬭⬭⬭⬭" ⬭⬭⬭⬭⬭⬭⬭

JUMBLE®

Unscramble these four Jumbles, one letter to each square, to form four ordinary words.

DASIT

BATOB

COPHON

PLUCUF

This will shut them up

WHEN HIS PALS MADE FUN OF HIS BALDNESS, HE----

Now arrange the circled letters to form the surprise answer, as suggested by the above cartoon.

Answer: ◯◯◯ A " ◯◯◯ " ◯◯ IT

JUMBLE®

Unscramble these four Jumbles, one letter to each square, to form four ordinary words.

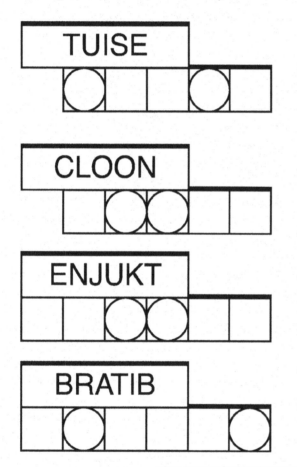

TUISE

CLOON

ENJUKT

BRATIB

Fill 'er up

Me, too

I'll be right with you

WHAT THE GAS STATION OWNER SAID WHEN HE WAS SWAMPED WITH BUSINESS.

Now arrange the circled letters to form the surprise answer, as suggested by the above cartoon.

Answer: " ◯◯◯◯◯ " A ◯◯◯

JUMBLE®

Unscramble these four Jumbles, one letter to each square, to form four ordinary words.

USHOE

DUGIE

WAYYAN

TYGODS

First, swab the deck...then....

WHEN THE SAILORS WERE AT SEA, THEY WERE---

Now arrange the circled letters to form the surprise answer, as suggested by the above cartoon.

A: ⬡⬡⬡⬡⬡ IN ⬡⬡⬡⬡⬡⬡⬡

JUMBLE®

Unscramble these four Jumbles, one letter to
each square, to form four ordinary words.

BREPO

MUBOX

LARCIA

HOCORB

Uncle Max made
beautiful rugs

WHAT THE WEAVER
LEFT IN HIS
ESTATE.

Now arrange the circled letters to form the
surprise answer, as suggested by the above
cartoon.

Answer: AN " ⬡⬡⬡⬡ " ⬡⬡⬡⬡

JUMBLE®

Unscramble these four Jumbles, one letter to
each square, to form four ordinary words.

DUSEE

ATTIR

HALIDA

HERNET

They're getting restless

Udders
are full

MOOOOO

HOW THE FARMER
KNEW THE COWS
WERE READY FOR
MILKING.

Now arrange the circled letters to form the
surprise answer, as suggested by the above
cartoon.

Ans: HE ⬭⬭⬭⬭⬭ THE ⬭⬭⬭⬭

JUMBLE®

Unscramble these four Jumbles, one letter to
each square, to form four ordinary words.

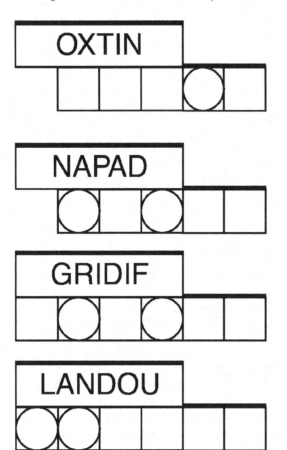

OXTIN

NAPAD

GRIDIF

LANDOU

They need to
be packed

WHAT FOLLOWS
WHEN PLUM TREES
ARE HARVESTED.

Now arrange the circled letters to form the
surprise answer, as suggested by the above
cartoon.

Print answer here: "  "

JUMBLE®

Unscramble these four Jumbles, one letter to
each square, to form four ordinary words.

DAPIL

VANIE

ANGLAR

GLEGGI

Third time
this week

WHEN THE TRAIN
WAS LATE, THE COM-
MUTERS WERE----

Now arrange the circled letters to form the
surprise answer, as suggested by the above
cartoon.

Print answer here: "  "

157

JUMBLE®

Unscramble these four Jumbles, one letter to
each square, to form four ordinary words.

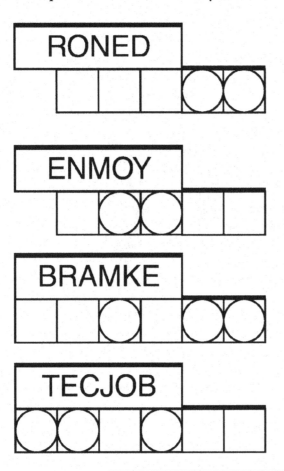

RONED

ENMOY

BRAMKE

TECJOB

I'm making a
cover for my
cast

CAN BE KNITTED
WHILE MENDING.

Now arrange the circled letters to form the
surprise answer, as suggested by the above
cartoon.

Ans: A ☐☐☐☐☐☐☐ ☐☐☐☐

JUMBLE

Unscramble these four Jumbles, one letter to each square, to form four ordinary words.

BATHI

FEACH

TIFFUL

MIRVEN

I'm catching up on my gardening and reading

WHAT THE MATH TEACHER ENJOYED WHEN SHE RETIRED.

Now arrange the circled letters to form the surprise answer, as suggested by the above cartoon.

A: THE " ◯◯◯◯◯◯-◯◯◯◯ "

JUMBLE

Unscramble these four Jumbles, one letter to
each square, to form four ordinary words.

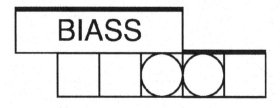

BIASS

ROARB

KLACEY

THEIRE

Cicero's
in the lead

FOLLOWED THE
HORSES IN
ANCIENT ROME.

Now arrange the circled letters to form the
surprise answer, as suggested by the above
cartoon.

Print answer here:

160

JUMBLE®

Unscramble these four Jumbles, one letter to
each square, to form four ordinary words.

NOGGI

SEUDO

BASURD

BOPHIS

It's all mine as far
as the eye can see

WHAT THE SUCCESS-
FUL RANCHER HAD.

Now arrange the circled letters to form the
surprise answer, as suggested by the above
cartoon.

Ans: A ⬡⬡⬡⬡ " ⬡⬡⬡⬡⬡⬡⬡ "

JUMBLE®

Unscramble these four Jumbles, one letter to
each square, to form four ordinary words.

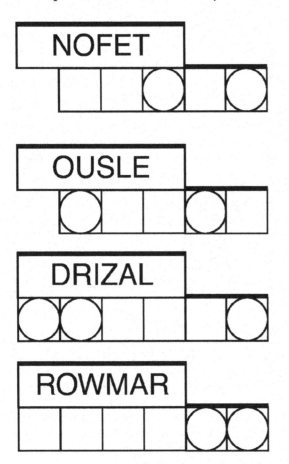

NOFET

OUSLE

DRIZAL

ROWMAR

So much
for that
old pillow

WHEN THE GOOSE
FEATHERS FLEW UP
AND AWAY, THEY
WERE----

Now arrange the circled letters to form the
surprise answer, as suggested by the above
cartoon.

Answer: " "

JUMBLE®

GALAXY

Challenger Puzzles

JUMBLE®

Unscramble these six Jumbles, one letter to each square, to form six ordinary words.

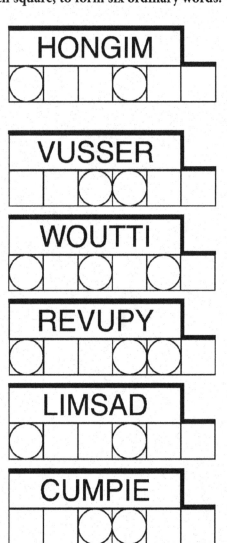

HONGIM

VUSSER

WOUTTI

REVUPY

LIMSAD

CUMPIE

I saw a ghost! Let's get out of here

WHY HE RAN OUT OF THE HAUNTED HOUSE.

Now arrange the circled letters to form the surprise answer, as suggested by the above cartoon.

Print answer here

THE "⬭⬭⬭⬭⬭⬭" ⬭⬭⬭⬭⬭ ⬭⬭⬭

JUMBLE®

Unscramble these six Jumbles, one letter to each square, to form six ordinary words.

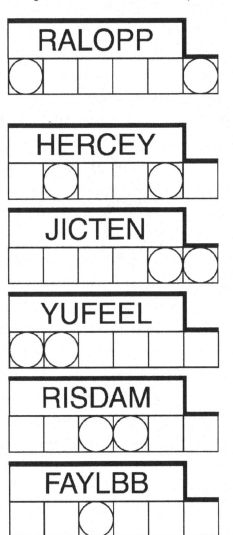

RALOPP

HERCEY

JICTEN

YUFEEL

RISDAM

FAYLBB

We still need a teapot lid

WHAT THE GROUP TURNED INTO WHEN THEY WENT ON A TREASURE HUNT.

Now arrange the circled letters to form the surprise answer, as suggested by the above cartoon.

Print answer here

A " ⬡⬡⬡⬡⬡⬡ " ⬡⬡⬡⬡⬡

JUMBLE

Unscramble these six Jumbles, one letter to each square, to form six ordinary words.

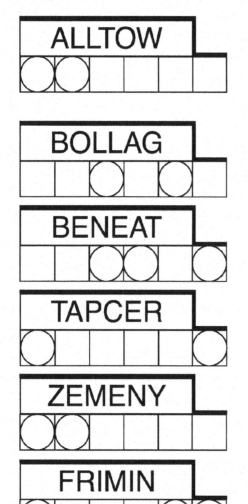

ALLTOW

BOLLAG

BENEAT

TAPCER

ZEMENY

FRIMIN

A lot of celebrities come here

WHEN THE MOVIE STAR WENT TO THE HAIRSTYLIST, HE BECAME THE---

Now arrange the circled letters to form the surprise answer, as suggested by the above cartoon.

Print answer here

JUMBLE

Unscramble these six Jumbles, one letter to
each square, to form six ordinary words.

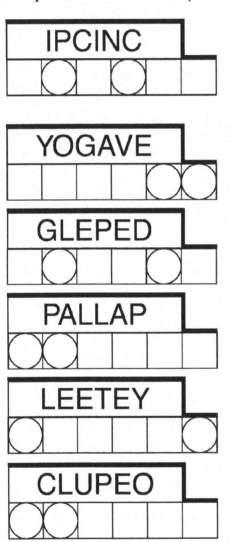

IPCINC

YOGAVE

GLEPED

PALLAP

LEETEY

CLUPEO

Light as a feather and
filled with taste

HOW THE DINING
CRITIC DESCRIBED
THE OMELET.

Now arrange the circled letters to form the
surprise answer, as suggested by the above
cartoon.

Print answer here

JUMBLE

Unscramble these six Jumbles, one letter to each square, to form six ordinary words.

BLIMER

BHLEED

MAGITS

NUGSUF

KRALTE

MILDIP

Gosh, I never expected this. I'm at a loss for words

WHEN HIS STATUE WAS UNVEILED, THE CIVIC LEADER WAS——

Now arrange the circled letters to form the surprise answer, as suggested by the above cartoon.

Print answer here

JUMBLE

Unscramble these six Jumbles, one letter to each square, to form six ordinary words.

CERAPH

CELEEF

MANDET

CHARNB

HUGONE

PROCEO

STRIKE THREE!

Take a seat, counselor

Oh, well, it's for a good cause

WHAT THE LAWYER DID AFTER STRIK- ING OUT IN THE CHARITY GAME.

Now arrange the circled letters to form the surprise answer, as suggested by the above cartoon.

Print answer here

◯◯◯◯◯◯◯◯◯◯◯◯ THE ◯◯◯◯◯◯

JUMBLE®

Unscramble these six Jumbles, one letter to each square, to form six ordinary words.

URBAUN

ANOMEY

SHEERY

YULNOH

DEAMOP

FIFRAM

You're number one in this and number one in that. It's always about you

SHE DECIDED TO DUMP THE EGOIST BECAUSE SHE----

Now arrange the circled letters to form the surprise answer, as suggested by the above cartoon.

Print answer here

JUMBLE®

Unscramble these six Jumbles, one letter to each square, to form six ordinary words.

NOOBBA

DINKAP

BETHIL

LAIHNE

HIMSUL

EMBLAG

My money worries are over

WHAT THE WINNER SAID WHEN HE COLLECTED HIS LOTTERY PRIZE.

Now arrange the circled letters to form the surprise answer, as suggested by the above cartoon.

Print answer here

A "

JUMBLE®

Unscramble these six Jumbles, one letter to each square, to form six ordinary words.

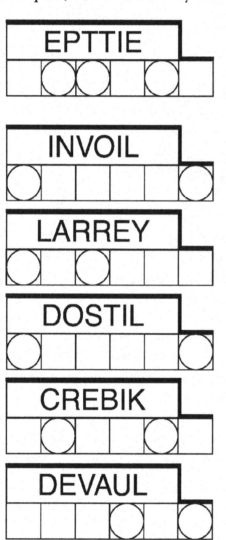

EPTTIE

INVOIL

LARREY

DOSTIL

CREBIK

DEVAUL

This is harder than it looks

PRO

WHEN THE GOLFER GOT A LESSON ON HOW TO TEE OFF, SHE BECAME A---

Now arrange the circled letters to form the surprise answer, as suggested by the above cartoon.

Print answer here

JUMBLE®

Unscramble these six Jumbles, one letter to
each square, to form six ordinary words.

NOBENT

GINBUL

MELVUL

CAINAM

TOOLEC

REECCO

That is one
ugly tie

A SHARP TONGUE
CAN LEAD TO
THIS.

Now arrange the circled letters to form the
surprise answer, as suggested by the above
cartoon.

Print answer here

A " ◯◯◯◯◯ " ◯◯◯◯◯◯◯◯

JUMBLE®

Unscramble these six Jumbles, one letter to
each square, to form six ordinary words.

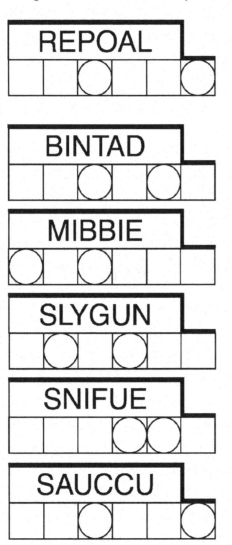

REPOAL

BINTAD

MIBBIE

SLYGUN

SNIFUE

SAUCCU

You're as red as
a lobster

I'm fine.
Just working
on my tan

WHEN MOM TOLD
THE TEEN TO GET
OUT OF THE SUN,
IT BECAME A----

Now arrange the circled letters to form the
surprise answer, as suggested by the above
cartoon.

Print answer here

“ ”

JUMBLE

Unscramble these six Jumbles, one letter to
each square, to form six ordinary words.

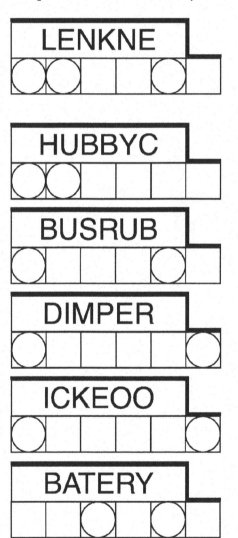

LENKNE

HUBBYC

BUSRUB

DIMPER

ICKEOO

BATERY

I was as wild as this
coat back then

HE WORE A PLAID
JACKET TO THE
FIFTIES PARTY
BECAUSE HE HAD A——

Now arrange the circled letters to form the
surprise answer, as suggested by the above
cartoon.

Print answer here

" "

JUMBLE®

Unscramble these six Jumbles, one letter to each square, to form six ordinary words.

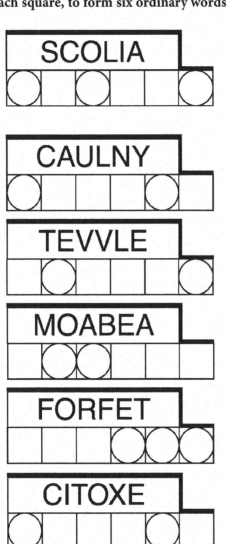

SCOLIA

CAULNY

TEVVLE

MOABEA

FORFET

CITOXE

Two thousand dollars?

The interest keeps growing

WHEN THE DEAD-BEATS WERE TRACKED DOWN, THE BILL WAS A----

Now arrange the circled letters to form the surprise answer, as suggested by the above cartoon.

Print answer here

" ⬡⬡⬡⬡⬡⬡⬡⬡' ⬡ " ⬡⬡⬡⬡

176

JUMBLE®

Unscramble these six Jumbles, one letter to each square, to form six ordinary words.

FEEDAM

INTERE

THOREX

BOADUN

JEERTS

STESUL

Drawing graffiti, Judge

Guilty. $500. Next.

WHAT THE VANDAL SAID WHEN HE WAS SENTENCED.

Now arrange the circled letters to form the surprise answer, as suggested by the above cartoon.

Print answer here

177

JUMBLE®

Unscramble these six Jumbles, one letter to
each square, to form six ordinary words.

WHOSAD

TIPIED

CANVAT

CLIPEN

WOAMED

CEADED

Check the
compass again

HOW THE HIKERS
TRAVERSED THE
RUSSIAN PLAINS.

Now arrange the circled letters to form the
surprise answer, as suggested by the above
cartoon.

Print answer here

AT
A

JUMBLE

Unscramble these six Jumbles, one letter to each square, to form six ordinary words.

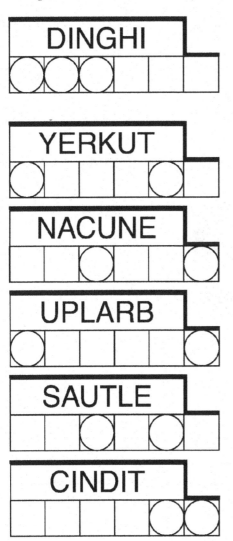

DINGHI

YERKUT

NACUNE

UPLARB

SAUTLE

CINDIT

It's gonna be a fight to the finish

WZYC

| VISITORS | 0 | 0 | 0 | 0 | 0 | 0 | | |
| HOME | 0 | 0 | 0 | 0 | 0 | 0 | | |

THE SCORELESS BASEBALL GAME TURNED INTO A----

Now arrange the circled letters to form the surprise answer, as suggested by the above cartoon.

Print answer here

" ◯◯◯◯◯◯◯ " ◯◯◯◯◯◯

JUMBLE®

Unscramble these six Jumbles, one letter to
each square, to form six ordinary words.

GRAFUL

BILGEO

STRYVE

CLIOCA

BLABED

RYCKIT

That few
miles took
a long
time

That'll be
$50

WHAT AN
UNSCRUPULOUS
CAB DRIVER CAN DO.

Now arrange the circled letters to form the
surprise answer, as suggested by the above
cartoon.

Print answer here

☐☐☐☐ ☐☐☐☐ ☐☐☐ A " ☐☐☐☐ "

180

JUMBLE®

Unscramble these six Jumbles, one letter to
each square, to form six ordinary words.

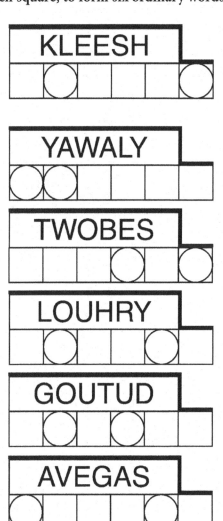

KLEESH

YAWALY

TWOBES

LOUHRY

GOUTUD

AVEGAS

I'll get
this

WHEN THE CHECK
ARRIVED, HIS
CLIENT'S TENDER
STEAK BECAME---

Now arrange the circled letters to form the
surprise answer, as suggested by the above
cartoon.

Print answer here

☐☐☐☐☐ TO ☐☐☐☐☐☐☐

JUMBLE®

Unscramble these six Jumbles, one letter to
each square, to form six ordinary words.

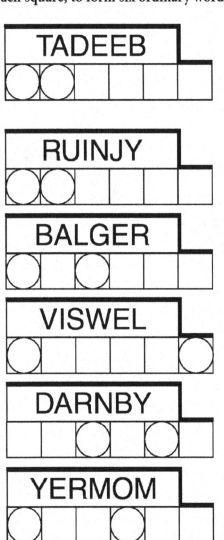

TADEEB

RUINJY

BALGER

VISWEL

DARNBY

YERMOM

Every day it's
"open, rinse"

THE DENTIST QUIT
HIS PRACTICE
BECAUSE IT WAS
THE---

Now arrange the circled letters to form the
surprise answer, as suggested by the above
cartoon.

Print answer here

JUMBLE®

Unscramble these six Jumbles, one letter to each square, to form six ordinary words.

RIMAPI

LARMON

ENGLOB

SCARFA

SMUCLY

BOBJER

It's as light as air

A WINNING CAKE RECIPE MUST DO THIS.

Now arrange the circled letters to form the surprise answer, as suggested by the above cartoon.

Print answer here

" ⃝⃝⃝⃝⃝ " TO THE ⃝⃝⃝⃝⃝⃝⃝⃝⃝

ANSWERS

1. **Jumbles:** SWOON FIORD BOYISH BAUBLE
   Answer: What they did when she pressed his shirt and he practiced his swing — USED IRONS

2. **Jumbles:** GAILY LUCID ACTING JAGUAR
   Answer: The accountant married her rich client because she was — CALCULATING

3. **Jumbles:** STOIC TYING GATHER INVEST
   Answer: What the bartender told the tipsy driver to do — SIT "TIGHT"

4. **Jumbles:** MOOSE SHEAF FONDLY ALIGHT
   Answer: What she did when the repairman got dirt on her carpet — TOLD HIM "OFF"

5. **Jumbles:** JOLLY RUMMY MURMUR HYBRID
   Answer: What Junior used when he helped Mom with the dishes — "DRY" HUMOR

6. **Jumbles:** CHAOS SLANT DEPICT UNTRUE
   Answer: What she wore to her yoga class — "STRETCH" PANTS

7. **Jumbles:** BLOOD LLAMA PAYOFF BEDBUG
   Answer: What it can take to rekindle a romance — AN OLD FLAME

8. **Jumbles:** SHINY PARTY ENGINE BLOUSE
   Answer: For the geometry class, the study of circles was — POINTLESS

9. **Jumbles:** TOKEN AGENT HECKLE DEAFEN
   Answer: Hemming dresses all day left the seamstress — ON THE "EDGE"

10. **Jumbles:** AORTA KNIFE WALRUS HOOKED
    Answer: When the spacecraft landed, the astronaut was — DOWN TO "EARTH"

11. **Jumbles:** TRACT THYME BRAZEN WEASEL
    Answer: When the clerk whispered to the customer over the counter, it was — BETWEEN THEM

12. **Jumbles:** DADDY AWOKE TONGUE ACCORD
    Answer: What the lawyer did for the house buyers — A GOOD "DEED"

13. **Jumbles:** GNOME RANCH BEFOUL GRIMLY
    Answer: What role did the child actress play in the movie? — A "MINOR" ONE

14. **Jumbles:** SWAMP NEWLY CATTLE MATRON
    Answer: When the hairdresser raised her fee, it was — "PERMANENT"

15. **Jumbles:** CRAWL FOAMY VORTEX MYRIAD
    Answer: What the college student faced when he went to the dentist — AN "ORAL" EXAM

16. **Jumbles:** GLAND MAJOR BECALM LAWYER
    Answer: When the acupuncture worked, the patient said it was — A JAB WELL DONE

17. **Jumbles:** BERET CHAMP CAUGHT MASCOT
    Answer: When the winning doubles partners wore the same outfits, it was — GAME, SET, "MATCH"

18. **Jumbles:** IRATE HEDGE SURELY DECEIT
    Answer: What the guidance counselor did when he picked up the hitchhiker — "STEERED" HIM RIGHT

19. **Jumbles:** PAUSE BORAX MYSTIC CODGER
    Answer: A judge will do this when he has a tennis match — GO TO "COURT"

20. **Jumbles:** LANKY BIPED POUNCE BEWAIL
    Answer: What the sleeping recruits felt like when they heard the bugle — BLOWN "UP"

21. **Jumbles:** EXUDE AMITY MUFFIN OVERDO
    Answer: What the piano player worked on — A "MOVEMENT"

22. **Jumbles:** ENSUE FLANK FILLET PRAYER
    Answer: What he saw when he visited the print shop — ALL "TYPES"

23. **Jumbles:** HAVEN BOGUS EFFACE FORGER
    Answer: What the brawlers faced when they were arrested for battery — "CHARGES"

24. **Jumbles:** COUPE PRONE REDEEM INTAKE
    Answer: What he did after the company farewell party — HE "RETIRED"

25. **Jumbles:** FEINT MINCE GAMBOL LARYNX
    Answer: Why Mom agreed to appear in the movie crowd scene — FOR "EXTRA" MONEY

26. **Jumbles:** FLAKE CHEEK JAGUAR DOUBLY
    Answer: The chef's new recipe failed because it was — HALF-BAKED

27. **Jumbles:** POKER CHAFF TRUSTY CROTCH
    Answer: What the tailor used to measure the bagpiper for his kilt — "SCOTCH" TAPE

28. **Jumbles:** SNACK VAGUE GRISLY PARISH
    Answer: What he used on a rainy day — HIS SAVINGS

29. **Jumbles:** RHYME RUSTY EQUITY SOIREE
    Answer: What an "uppity" waiter is bound to get — A "RISE" OUT OF THEM

30. **Jumbles:** NOTCH HENNA CHARGE BISHOP
    Answer: When he entered the costume contest, he didn't have a — "GHOST" OF A CHANCE

31. **Jumbles:** DECAY ASSAY RAMROD FALTER
    Answer: When the astronomy students finished studying, they were — "STARRY" EYED

32. **Jumbles:** CHOKE STOKE TRUISM CIPHER
    Answer: What she experienced when she shopped for a cactus plant — "STICKER" SHOCK

33. **Jumbles:** GAUGE ABYSS POPLIN MAGPIE
    Answer: Why the senator didn't submit his report — A "PAGE" WAS MISSING

34. **Jumbles:** SHYLY AGONY TAWDRY SUNDAE
    Answer: Why the editor rejected the italic headline — IT WAS "SLANTED"

35. **Jumbles:** WHEAT LATHE INSIST GARISH
    Answer: What the opera singer did when she took the ocean voyage — HIT THE HIGH "SEAS"

36. **Jumbles:** FINIS GLAND FOSSIL ATTAIN
    Answer: What Dad faced when he bought a balloon — INFLATION

37. **Jumbles:** ABOVE CLUCK FAMOUS SEPTIC
    Answer: A good way to secure housing — USE LOCKS

38. **Jumbles:** SWISH TRUTH LAVISH CRAFTY
    Answer: What the jockey said when the perennial also-ran won the race — THAT WAS A "FIRST"

39. **Jumbles:** SKULK METAL WAITER IMPEDE
    Answer: What happened when the thieves ran into the cornfield? — THEY WERE "STALKED"

40. **Jumbles:** TULLE WEIGH BUCKET CENSUS
    Answer: When the sewing club watched the comedy show, they were — IN "STITCHES"

41. **Jumbles:** PEACE MIRTH TIMELY ANKLET
    Answer: The owner of a candy factory can do this — MAKE A "MINT"

42. **Jumbles:** OWING AWARD STANZA PODIUM
    Answer: An artist and a horse can do this — "DRAW" A WAGON

43. **Jumbles:** RAPID HURRY BAMBOO JOYOUS
    Answer: What the neighbors shared in the laundry room — "DRY" HUMOR

44. **Jumbles:** ENVOY LINGO EXPEND NOZZLE
    Answer: Watching football all day can affect your — "END" ZONE

45. **Jumbles:** WINCE LARVA RADIUS MAKEUP
    Answer: The new sailor took the upper bunk because he didn't want to — MAKE WAVES

46. **Jumbles:** CABIN BULGY LETHAL PSYCHE
    Answer: When the scientists met on a cross-country flight, they talked on — A HIGH "PLANE"

47. **Jumbles:** HATCH ENEMY TYRANT EGOISM
Answer: What the Italian fisherman said when he snared an eel in his net — "THAT'S A MORAY"

48. **Jumbles:** GUISE FISHY AWEIGH BEHIND
Answer: What the excavator enjoyed when his house was finished — HIS NEW "DIGS"

49. **Jumbles:** REARM PAGAN ORATOR FIERCE
Answer: When the bumper corn crop left the farmer grinning, it was — FROM EAR TO EAR

50. **Jumbles:** FAULT ABBEY CALIPH AROUND
Answer: When the trick failed, the magician wanted to — PULL HIS HARE OUT

51. **Jumbles:** PIECE BEIGE ENJOIN PRIMER
Answer: To many, when marriage is mentioned, it has a — NICE "RING" TO IT

52. **Jumbles:** MANGY PUPPY PAYING JINGLE
Answer: When he lost the case, the handsome lawyer was — "APPEALING"

53. **Jumbles:** TRILL AIDED LOCKET TYCOON
Answer: What Junior got when he came home filthy — A "DIRTY" LOOK

54. **Jumbles:** FETCH NOVEL AGHAST NAUGHT
Answer: What she got when she dried her laundry outdoors — THE "HANG" OF IT

55. **Jumbles:** ITCHY AUGUR METRIC ANEMIA
Answer: When pantyhose went on sale, there was a — "RUN" ON THEM

56. **Jumbles:** LOWLY EXTOL WIDEST DISCUS
Answer: Why the nattily-dressed player won the bridge hand — HE WAS WELL "SUITED"

57. **Jumbles:** LYING BOUND CAJOLE CHROME
Answer: What the boss did in the doughnut shop — THE "HOLE" JOB

58. **Jumbles:** SNOWY CROWN WEAKEN AUTHOR
Answer: What might a taxi driver use to trim his trees — A "HACK" SAW

59. **Jumbles:** ARMOR CUBIC ACCENT NAUSEA
Answer: Easy to get when one trains — A STRAIN

60. **Jumbles:** BELIE SORRY ABACUS JUMBLE
Answer: Why the mobster's tailor quit — IT WAS A "SEAMY" JOB

61. **Jumbles:** KINKY KNACK GAMBIT STUCCO
Answer: What the giant wrestler was interested in when he read the menu — CONSUMING

62. **Jumbles:** RIGOR HAIRY BOTHER MUSKET
Answer: She married the know-it-all because he was — MR. "RIGHT"

63. **Jumbles:** MAKER HAVOC INLAND TRYING
Answer: When the nuclear scientist turned on the car stereo, he was — RADIO ACTIVE

64. **Jumbles:** BALMY NATAL UNPACK APIECE
Answer: Often spotted in a fancy restaurant — A NAPKIN

65. **Jumbles:** CLOUT BRAIN BUTTON MOROSE
Answer: When the heavyweight champ was interviewed, it was — ABOUT A BOUT

66. **Jumbles:** UPPER GOOSE DROPSY ENTAIL
Answer: Sounds like what they discussed — DISGUST

67. **Jumbles:** PIPER TOPAZ GENDER POWDER
Answer: Why his pals were like ice cubes — THEY "DROPPED" IN

68. **Jumbles:** CHIME DIZZY EMBALM MANAGE
Answer: When the little Indians got lost, the cornfield became a — MAIZE MAZE

69. **Jumbles:** FLOOR EJECT POLISH FIDDLE
Answer: What happened when she went out with the air-conditioning salesman — HE LEFT HER "COLD"

70. **Jumbles:** ADAPT ELATE FROSTY GOPHER
Answer: Always a possessive indication — AN APOSTROPHE

71. **Jumbles:** FROZE LUSTY JIGGLE TEACUP
Answer: What the boss did when he went to bed facing a big decision — "SLEPT" ON IT

72. **Jumbles:** FIFTY EXCEL CORNEA INVITE
Answer: Any way you look at it, this pertains to a city — CIVIC

73. **Jumbles:** FLOUT EMERY SUBTLY SEAMAN
Answer: What the horse breeder considered her husband — A "STABLE" MATE

74. **Jumbles:** AFOOT FAIRY JAILED BECKON
Answer: What Dad considered the icy drink on a hot day — A COOL "AID"

75. **Jumbles:** BYLAW HAREM FERRET CAMPER
Answer: A good place to find a date — A PALM TREE

76. **Jumbles:** JUICE ANNOY HANGER FIRING
Answer: What Mom will do when the kids object to Dad's shower singing — JOIN THE "REFRAIN"

77. **Jumbles:** FLUKE VALET WOBBLE SULTRY
Answer: Can be heard at a snooty garden party — "FLOWERY" TALK

78. **Jumbles:** HUSKY SMACK MARKUP POLICY
Answer: Another name for a lullaby — "ROCK" MUSIC

79. **Jumbles:** SUAVE FLUID NOODLE CABANA
Answer: When the sailor didn't tie the rope properly, it was — "BOUND" TO FAIL

80. **Jumbles:** EXPEL WHOOP NOGGIN DIGEST
Answer: What happened when the teenager polished Dad's car — HE "SHINED"

81. **Jumbles:** SOOTY PHONY ASYLUM MEDLEY
Answer: What the dairy farmer milked when he was kicked by old Betsy — SYMPATHY

82. **Jumbles:** LATCH GUESS ROTATE ERMINE
Answer: What the tourists paid to use a cell phone in Italy — "ROMAN" CHARGES

83. **Jumbles:** BANJO IMBUE REFUGE VACUUM
Answer: When the smoke-belching jalopy went by, the pedestrians were — "FUMING"

84. **Jumbles:** SINGE TEPID ICEBOX NEGATE
Answer: The burly wrestler refused acupuncture because he didn't want to — GET "PINNED"

85. **Jumbles:** COACH BANAL MODEST SYMBOL
Answer: This happens before the Fourth of July — SALES "BOOM"

86. **Jumbles:** DALLY DUMPY BURIAL WEAPON
Answer: Where hubby ended up on his day off — UP THE WALL

87. **Jumbles:** OLDER HEAVY PERMIT POROUS
Answer: How the cosmetics student arrived at the right answer — SHE "MADE IT UP"

88. **Jumbles:** DAILY ELITE FLIMSY FABLED
Answer: What the movie about the moonshiner turned into — A "STILL" LIFE

89. **Jumbles:** BROOD COMET ADAGIO FAMISH
Answer: The kids turned the abandoned recliner into a — "CHAIR-IOT"

90. **Jumbles:** TACKY RURAL TANGLE FORKED
Answer: What the hot dog vendor gave his new helper — "FRANK" TALK

91. **Jumbles:** EVOKE FOLIO SPONGE TRAGIC
Answer: How the hikers described the campsite overlooking the canyons — "GORGES"

92. **Jumbles:** UNITY ROBOT GAIETY BANNER
Answer: What he paid when he went to driving school — ATTENTION

93. **Jumbles:** MERGE TWINE SEETHE IMPACT
Answer: Developing a pot belly over the years is a — "WAIST" OF TIME

94. **Jumbles:** FOYER BEFIT FROTHY REBUKE
Answer: How the tenderfoot felt when he fell from the horse after the long ride — BETTER "OFF"

95. **Jumbles:** PUPIL TRYST JUNGLE IMPEND
Answer: Where the dog slept when the family went camping — IN THE "PUP" TENT

96. **Jumbles:** SNORT BRINY YEARLY TOWARD
Answer: What happened when the cowboy caused trouble at the saloon — HE WAS "BARRED"

97. **Jumbles:** BROOK AGILE OBLONG QUEASY
Answer: Discounted happy hour drinks can result in — "BAR-GAINS"

98. **Jumbles:** CARGO YACHT LAWFUL DEBTOR
Answer: What the couple learned when they took singing lessons — HOW TO "DUET"

99. **Jumbles:** NEWSY CRACK HARDLY SCORCH
Answer: Why the con man planted trees in his back yard — IT WAS "SHADY" WORK

100. **Jumbles:** MILKY CHALK ENCAMP BUOYED
Answer: When he lost the chess game, he — PAID BY "CHECK"

101. **Jumbles:** HEDGE MUSIC JOYFUL ALPACA
Answer: How he paid for the freezer — "COLD" CASH

102. **Jumbles:** LOUSY IRATE CANYON WALLOP
Answer: How the model felt after the long fashion show — "WORN" OUT

103. **Jumbles:** CUBIT POUCH BROKEN COMPEL
Answer: When the diner said, "Well done," he wasn't praising — THE COOK

104. **Jumbles:** DRYLY ABATE MEASLY NATURE
Answer: When she modeled the skimpy beachwear, she was — "BARELY" SEEN

105. **Jumbles:** SIXTY AZURE WEEVIL EYELID
Answer: The sharp dresser got the job at the men's store because he was — WELL-"SUITED"

106. **Jumbles:** FELON GIANT COUGAR HOOKED
Answer: Why the prisoner visited the barber — TO GET "UNLOCKED"

107. **Jumbles:** LIGHT AROMA DETAIN GASKET
Answer: What the pupils experienced when they failed the multiplication test — HARD "TIMES"

108. **Jumbles:** KETCH CEASE BUSILY SYSTEM
Answer: What the concert pianist considered his piano — HIS "KEYS" TO SUCCESS

109. **Jumbles:** GUARD DAISY KIMONO THEORY
Answer: When the researcher completed his earthquake study, he was — ON "SHAKY" GROUND

110. **Jumbles:** FLOOD PECAN ABRUPT COWARD
Answer: What the tax-dodging locksmith did when the IRS arrived — HE "BOLTED"

111. **Jumbles:** QUAIL FRAUD ISLAND INFLUX
Answer: He bought a round for the house because he had — "LIQUID" FUNDS

112. **Jumbles:** FOCUS GUILD LIKELY HANDED
Answer: When the mogul paid for his bust, he was — "CHISELED"

113. **Jumbles:** PAPER KNAVE COMPLY FEDORA
Answer: A good thing to have when playing a bridge hand — A "POKER" FACE

114. **Jumbles:** GUISE FISHY AWEIGH BEHIND
Answer: What the excavator enjoyed when his house was finished — HIS NEW "DIGS"

115. **Jumbles:** LILAC CAMEO GIMLET CYMBAL
Answer: What the postman delivered to the bachelor — MALE MAIL

116. **Jumbles:** YODEL FILMY JUSTLY SNAPPY
Answer: How the hunter stalked his prey when he lost his rifle scope — "AIMLESSLY"

117. **Jumbles:** TROTH BEGOT FEWEST DEFINE
Answer: What the dieter looked for when he got on the scale — A BETTER "WEIGH"

118. **Jumbles:** JOKER MOURN CHALET OMELET
Answer: What the server accessed on his computer — THE "MENU"

119. **Jumbles:** KNOWN SANDY STRONG KNOTTY
Answer: What he did while sitting — TOOK A "STAND"

120. **Jumbles:** FETID LINER INVOKE PLOWED
Answer: Why he wasn't afraid to go to the dentist — HE KNEW THE "DRILL"

121. **Jumbles:** GROOM ANISE FIZZLE PARLOR
Answer: A good way to better your lot —SELL IT FOR MORE

122. **Jumbles:** HAZEL VERVE HARROW RADISH
Answer: What the girl got when they frolicked in the ocean — "WAVES" IN HER HAIR

123. **Jumbles:** SQUAB EXACT FORBID HAZING
Answer: The couple was always in debt because they couldn't — "BUDGE IT"

124. **Jumbles:** BOOTY SCARF BENIGN ARCTIC
Answer: When the financier studied the merger, he found it — "ABSORBING"

125. **Jumbles:** SHAKY AXIOM BRUTAL NUTRIA
Answer: When he was named "watchmaker of the year," he became the — MAN OF THE "HOUR"

126. **Jumbles:** HEFTY JADED FESTAL MISERY
Answer: The marooned theatergoer finally got a — SEAT ON THE ISLE

127. **Jumbles:** MADAM CHAIR GAINED WEDGED
Answer: How the overworked seamstress felt — "HEMMED" IN

128. **Jumbles:** LADLE SHEEP ABUSED CLOVEN
Answer: What the barber experienced on his way to work — A CLOSE "SHAVE"

129. **Jumbles:** BUMPY MAXIM GUNNER VIRTUE
Answer: What the judge considered the high-profile case — "TRYING"

130. **Jumbles:** PRINT CRAFT ZINNIA GOBLET
Answer: What the sidewalk artist drew — ATTENTION

131. **Jumbles:** JUDGE HOBBY AGENDA FLURRY
Answer: What the poker player did when he helped with the laundry — HE "FOLDED"

132. **Jumbles:** USURY CYCLE HORROR DAMASK
Answer: When he lost the hot air balloon race, he became a — "SOAR" LOSER

133. **Jumbles:** FACET COWER SOOTHE ADJUST
Answer: What happened to the rumor of free drinks? — IT WAS "SCOTCHED"

134. **Jumbles:** BURST TUNED ANGINA QUIVER
Answer: What the gym boxers used to go for a couple of "rounds" — A "SQUARE" RING

135. **Jumbles:** ONION VIGIL PEOPLE GROTTO
Answer: When his dog had puppies, the street cleaner said it was — "LITTERING"

136. **Jumbles:** GASSY WRATH CATCHY EXPOSE
Answer: Although the lanky basketball player was long on talent, he was — "SHORT" ON CASH

137. **Jumbles:** DERBY LIVEN UPROAR BEMOAN
Answer: What the pro wrestler got when he won the match — "PIN" MONEY

138. **Jumbles:** BROIL MOSSY WISELY MAGNET
Answer: How he performed in the lifeguard test — "SWIMMINGLY"

139. **Jumbles:** RAINY OCTET TWINGE PIGPEN
Answer: When rain hits a picnic, it can — "WET" AN APPETITE

140. **Jumbles:** PROVE MADLY GENTLE WHALER
Answer: When his wife stormed out after their -argument, she took — HER "LEAVE"

141. **Jumbles:** BASIN LOGIC WHOLLY IMPOSE
Answer: Where to find runners-up no matter who wins the race — ON A HILL CLIMB

142. **Jumbles:** PANIC SLANT GEYSER WIZARD
Answer: At the end of the day, the plumber's new helper said the work was — "DRAINING"

143. **Jumbles:** VENOM ENACT JERSEY PILFER
Answer: What a "present" can be — A SERPENT

144. **Jumbles:** DOUGH AGING MUSCLE INCOME
Answer: To some, an interest in food can be — "CONSUMING"

145. **Jumbles:** ALBUM TAKEN DENTAL PLURAL
Answer: What the sharp dresser turned out to be —
A "DULL" TALKER

146. **Jumbles:** EIGHT DOGMA SCHEME FACING
Answer: What the cops did when they questioned the
crooner — MADE HIM "SING"

147. **Jumbles:** COVEY DUCAT ANYHOW HERMIT
Answer: When the retiree was honored with a gold watch, he
became the —MAN OF THE HOUR

148. **Jumbles:** JUROR MUSTY HICCUP FLATLY
Answer: What the knife thrower wore on stage —
A "SHARP" OUTFIT

149. **Jumbles:** STAID ABBOT PONCHO CUPFUL
Answer: When his pals made fun of his baldness, he —
PUT A "LID" ON IT

150. **Jumbles:** SUITE COLON JUNKET RABBIT
Answer: What the gas station owner said when he was
swamped with business — "TANKS" A LOT

151. **Jumbles:** HOUSE GUIDE ANYWAY STODGY
Answer: When the sailors were at sea, they were —
AWASH IN DUTIES

152. **Jumbles:** PROBE BUXOM RACIAL BROOCH
Answer: What the weaver left in his estate —
AN "HEIR" LOOM

153. **Jumbles:** SUEDE TRAIT DAHLIA NETHER
Answer: How the farmer knew the cows were ready for
milking — HE HEARD THE HERD

154. **Jumbles:** TOXIN PANDA FRIGID UNLOAD
Answer: What follows when plum trees are harvested —
"PRUNING"

155. **Jumbles:** PLAID NAÏVE RAGLAN GIGGLE
Answer: When the train was late, the commuters were —
"RAILING"

156. **Jumbles:** DRONE MONEY EMBARK OBJECT
Answer: Can be knitted while mending — A BROKEN BONE

157. **Jumbles:** HABIT CHAFE FITFUL VERMIN
Answer: What the math teacher enjoyed when she retired —
THE "AFTER-MATH"

158. **Jumbles:** BASIS ARBOR LACKEY EITHER
Answer: Followed the horses in ancient Rome — CHARIOTS

159. **Jumbles:** GOING DOUSE ABSURD BISHOP
Answer: What the successful rancher had — A BIG "SPREAD"

160. **Jumbles:** OFTEN LOUSE LIZARD MARROW
Answer: When the goose feathers flew up and away, they
were — STILL "DOWN"

161. **Jumbles:** HOMING VERSUS OUTWIT PURVEY DISMAL
PUMICE
Answer: Why he ran out of the haunted house —
THE "SPIRIT" MOVED HIM

162. **Jumbles:** POPLAR CHEERY INJECT EYEFUL DISARM FLABBY
Answer: What the group turned into when they went on a
treasure hunt — A "SEARCH" PARTY

163. **Jumbles:** TALLOW GLOBAL BEATEN CARPET ENZYME
INFIRM
Answer: When the movie star went to the hairstylist, he
became the — "MANE" ATTRACTION

164. **Jumbles:** PICNIC VOYAGE PLEDGE APPALL EYELET COUPLE
Answer: How the dining critic described the omelet —
"EGG-CEPTIONAL"

165. **Jumbles:** LIMBER BEHELD STIGMA FUNGUS TALKER
LIMPID
Answer: When his statue was unveiled, the civic leader
was — BESIDE HIMSELF

166. **Jumbles:** PREACH FLEECE TANDEM BRANCH ENOUGH
COOPER
Answer: What the lawyer did after striking out in the charity
game — APPROACHED THE BENCH

167. **Jumbles:** AUBURN YEOMAN HERESY UNHOLY POMADE
AFFIRM
Answer: She decided to dump the egoist because she —
HAD HIS NUMBER

168. **Jumbles:** BABOON KIDNAP BLITHE INHALE MULISH
GAMBLE
Answer: What the winner said when he collected his lottery
prize — THANKS A "MILLION"

169. **Jumbles:** PETITE VIOLIN RARELY STOLID BICKER VALUED
Answer: When the golfer got a lesson on how to tee off, she
became a — STUDENT "DRIVER"

170. **Jumbles:** BONNET BLUING VELLUM MANIAC OCELOT
COERCE
Answer: A sharp tongue can lead to this —
A "BLUNT" COMMENT

171. **Jumbles:** PAROLE BANDIT IMBIBE SNUGLY INFUSE
CAUCUS
Answer: When Mom told the teen to get out of the sun, it
became a — "BURNING" ISSUE

172. **Jumbles:** KENNEL CHUBBY SUBURB PRIMED COOKIE
BETRAY
Answer: He wore a plaid jacket to the fifties party because he
had a — "CHECKERED" PAST

173. **Jumbles:** SOCIAL LUNACY VELVET AMOEBA EFFORT
EXOTIC
Answer: When the deadbeats were tracked down, the bill
was a — "COLLECTOR'S" ITEM

174. **Jumbles:** DEFAME ENTIRE EXHORT ABOUND JESTER
TUSSLE
Answer: What the vandal said when he was sentenced —
THAT'S JUST "FINE"

175. **Jumbles:** SHADOW PITIED VACANT PENCIL MEADOW
DECADE
Answer: How the hikers traversed the Russian plains —
ONE STEPPE AT A TIME

176. **Jumbles:** HIDING TURKEY NUANCE BURLAP SALUTE
INDICT
Answer: The scoreless baseball game turned into a —
"PITCHED" BATTLE

177. **Jumbles:** FRUGAL OBLIGE VESTRY CALICO DABBLE TRICKY
Answer: What an unscrupulous cab driver can do —
TAKE YOU FOR A "RIDE"

178. **Jumbles:** SHEKEL WAYLAY BESTOW HOURLY DUGOUT
SAVAGE
Answer: When the check arrived, his client's tender steak
became — TOUGH TO SWALLOW

179. **Jumbles:** DEBATE INJURY GARBLE SWIVEL BRANDY
MEMORY
Answer: The dentist quit his practice because it was the —
SAME OLD "GRIND"

180. **Jumbles:** IMPAIR NORMAL BELONG FRACAS CLUMSY
JOBBER
Answer: A winning cake recipe must do this —
"RISE" TO THE OCCASION